The
Prince
of
Kokomo

T0106982

BOOKS BY LAINI MATAKA

Never As Strangers
Restoring the Queen
Bein A Strong Black Woman Can Get U Killed!!

poems

The Prince *of* Kokomo

LAINI MATAKA

BLACK CLASSIC PRESS
Baltimore

Copyright 2011 Laini Mataka

Published 2011 Black Classic Press
All Rights Reserved.
Library of Congress Control Number: 2010941860
ISBN: 978-1-57478-046-8

Cover art: *What about Adam* (Dedicated to Marshall Eddie Conway)
    by Julee Dickerson
Book Design: Guenet Abraham

Printed by BCP Digital Printing,
an affiliate company of Black Classic Press, Inc.

To review or purchase Black Classic Press books, visit:
www.blackclassicbooks.com

You may also obtain a list of titles by writing to:
Black Classic Press
c/o List
P.O. Box 13414
Baltimore, MD 21203

To the new stars in my ancestral skies:
Trunita Jackson, Steven Robinson,
Arsell Robinson Sr., Defelther Robinson Sr.,
Ronney Tyson, Dr. Asa Hilliard,
Mamadi Nyasuma, Rabiah Rayford,
Dr. Prem Deben, Brother Bey,
Ambrose Lane Sr., Ron Walters,
John H. Franklin, Michael Jackson,
Dorothy Height, Abbey Lincoln,
Max Roach, and Ainah D. Sneed.

love and gratitude go out to the following:
Mwalimu Baruti, Nana Kwabena Brown,
Nana Iya Marie, Alice Katina Thomas,
Aza Smith, Nia Turner, Nightwolf,
Haki Madhubuti, the Blue Nile,
the House of Khamit, Sankofa Videos and Books,
and the African Heritage Drummers and Dancers.

contents

The Prince of Kokomo

poems

for yr
information

the main thrust of the civil rights movement
was the lynching of willie lynch & all his descendants.
they had us boogaloo-ing & finger-popping to the tune of
if u're white, u're alright, if u're brown/stick around
if u're yellow, u're mellow, if u're blk/get back!

be deep chocolate & act like u were getting ready
to look a wite man in the eye & u cld lose yr
toilet cleaning privileges & be wite-balled away
from all opportunities to cut a slave.
be high yella & forget that wite only
was not a metaphor for u & yr head cld be opened up with
        a bully club
while yr body'd be dragged through the street and thrown
        into a jail
where the grand wizard was moonlighting as sheriff.
be a bubbling,
brown sugar seen talking to one of those naacp-ers,
        & u cld end up
being attacked by rabid dogs on two legs or four.

so they met secretly in each others' homes, with fear standing
        guard at one entrance and anticipation at the other.
they conspired in heated whispers/vascillating between victory
        & defeat. they were ordinary people tapping into the
        greatness of their own past. an act so sanctified & cohesive,
        it brought forth a river of supportive ancestors who'd been
        missing in action since slavery.
they took the certainty of their creator & wore it like velcro
        against blue eyes that vomited hatred all over their deepest
        yearnings.

LAINI MATAKA

for yr
information *(continued)*

the real work took place when the andrew youngs & jesse jacksons
   weren't anywhere in sight. the real muscle came from family
   members like yours that no one ever talks about anymore.
folks who didn't have a dollar,
but gave two to get strangers out of jail.
folks who, though tired of being afraid, took to the streets even
   though they knew they'd wind up crushed between concrete
   walls & the paralyzing water of industrial strength hoses. folks
   who were so committed to extracting beauty outa all that ugly,
   that their slightest word or deed cld bring about the death of
   everyone they loved.

if the every day negro hadn't taken such gargantuan risks, tommies
   mith and john carlos might never have saluted the olympics
   with clenched fists. if some anonymous black man hadn't been
   able to lift his head despite the redneck spit on his face, huey
   newton wouldn't have said anything & bobby seale wldn't have
   done anything. if the colored ministers/touched by the divine,
   hadn't turned their churches into war-rooms for anti-racist
   strategizing, even today's most renown minister wld still be
   churning out calypso songs.

some of the most dauntless everyday people took on the most
   perilous odds, so their descendant's cld later brag about
   being thugs:
with no resumes.
manicured gansta's & marshmallow filled rappers, talk outa their
   butts about everything but a way to end racism.
if they really wanna pay their dues, they need to jump into their
   overly-priced dummy-mobiles, & take a soldier's ride down to
   one of those little southern towns where jim crow is dead, but

jim jr. still has a strangle-hold on the black & beautiful.
let us make a new decree: that the only way u can be a thug, is
    to jack-up a klansman & take possession of his sheet, in
    alabama, in broad daylight.

for anyone who thinks the quest for civil rights was about uncle
    toms beggin for crumbs from whitey's table, answer this:
    have u ever given yr time, energy, genius, or love to a blk
    anything with no possibility of personal gain?
have u ever whispered thanx to the shoulders yr $200 nikes
    stand on
& did it ever occur to u that w/out the movement & dr. king
there's no way on earth u'd have all that bling, bling?

LAINI MATAKA

black love

is an intrepid metaphor
that selected spiritual beings live & die to honor.
'tis the breast milk of volcanoes
declaring itself in the exploding luminosity of pulsating beings.
black love, the gift God gave herself
is directly responsible
for heaven's burnished thighs opening
and humanity
oozing out.

black love

feel it against yr lips like a kiss
listen to the way the earth begs for its resurgence
on a scale of Maat, weigh it against
wite supremacy & watch the wicked
wage worldwide war to exclude
black love from humanity's agenda,
before it takes its rightful place
as the most redeeming force
on this precarious planet.

black love

is on the endangered species list, along with
common sense & virtue.
blk babies are falling outa blk wombs quicker than
blk hands can catch them.
young blk men spend more time romancing their cellmates
than their soul-mates.
while distrust jacks up the community

THE PRINCE OF KOKOMO

worse than election fraud.
black love is under major attack
& that in itself wldnt be so wretched if
some of the attackers werent also blk.

black love

has been so marginalized,
scrutinized, criticized and pulverized
been declared dead by a whole global system
when in fact it's
just as self-perpetuating as ever.
its genetic representatives are conjuring it up
faster than the u.s. can steal oil from Iraq .
black love is alive & about to kick hatred's ass
from the halls of Montezuma to the shores of Tripoli .
self-preservation is the only thing it knows
but the only thing it wants/is to reign in blk hearts.

LAINI MATAKA

et
tu conye

an enigma
for a moment only
& then we saw u all wrapped up in that
red white & blue
drinking pepsi
like u care about blk people.

nitwit tom on mathematics

massah jefferson sd
blacks were naturally inferior
in math.
      i bet

blk sally cld calculate how many times
she had to let her half-sister's
slave-holding husband
erase her age
with his semen.

LAINI MATAKA

green card
indictments

U come here
Knowing we're here.
U come here
Ignoring our condition
U come here
To feed us liquor
& seven/elevens of poison.
U come here
Looking at us through brown eyes,
Turned blue
As eager to exploit
As the Italians who turned u out.
U come here
Constantly aware of faces
That look just like those at home
yet
U come here
Bringing us no sense at all of
The afrikan warmth we've heard about.
U come here
But
U leave yr ethnic clothes at home
on the floor/
next to yr afrikan identity.

THE PRINCE OF KOKOMO

salty papa

2 unevolved
2 be confused enuff
2 be embarrassed
about boldly adoring his daddy
he became an ocean;
& his daddy/a real cool cat
with an aversion to water
was forced to seek the higher ground
of somebody else's mama.
junior
learned to hate water
& turned into a real salty-papa.
they say once,
he even made bessie smith
cry.

LAINI MATAKA

the
widow-mommies

meticulously coiffed,
& stretching denim to the limit
they travel in manicured packs
as if goaded by some imperceptible force;
pushing BMW strollers
decked with gadgetry/designed for pageantry.
they steer their squirming trophies
straight into a future that's walking backwards.
when their offspring cry, they nurse them
with screams left over from their
truncated youth.

the journey of the sun from east to west always
catches them trespassing on somebody else's
dream come true.
wherever they are
amusement parks spring up
liquor stores sing & chinese joints dance
their daily revelations revolve around a blunt
big enuff to blunt all pain.
their gossip is cyclical and all inclusive.
their estrogen keeps the air in a chokehold.
while on the otha side of the world, across the street,
the absentee daddies anoint themselves with 40's,
noses & tails already pointing towards new.

THE PRINCE OF KOKOMO

i
confess...

when i was young
i was
too chicken to be a Panther
being cats
i thought they'd eat me.

.

mr. 2,000 black
gets his due

(FOR MAMADI NYASUMA)

every time i cry, my third eye fills with images of an immense
hall shimmering in the purity of untainted sunlight,
a space of reckoning for blacknificent soldiers.
ethereal in its beauty, mystifying in its serenity, the hall of justice
reaches back into our deepest, darkest ancestry.
with a hot pepper preciseness i've never known,
i hear djembes screaming out the seriousness of yr presence;
i see u gliding down that hallway, clean to the bone,
flanked by ancestors on both sides.
faces u've loved, studied, envied, praised & never dreamt of seeing,
come rushing towards u, spilling over with unrestrained joy.
i see damu reaching out to give u some dap & barnett anxiously
slappin yr back as yr soulful strut proceeds, & u freeze
because u cant believe, that mongo and olatunji are rubbing dollars
all over yr face. yr elation becomes palpable/when from outa
        the mist malcolm & dr. clarke insist upon embracing u.
yr knees buckle, but amos wilson catches u,
queen mother moore
gets up from her throne to bring water to u
while the life u've just lived, starts releasing u.
i hear a host of angelic voices wailing in the background,
but i can't decipher the words, becuz its not my journey.
i feel the tumultuous stir as divine apparitions shift to make
        room for u.

i hear the heart-felt crescendo of applause wrapping itself
        around u
as the afrikans u were once torn from recapture and salute u.
but most of all, i hear the bursting of my own heart as it momen-
        tarily stumbles around in the grand canyon yr home-going
        created.

THE PRINCE OF KOKOMO

i'd like to scream and holla and roll around on the ground
but i can't. i'd like to blame someone, or hire a lawyer to take
    fate to court, but i can't. i'd like to break-down and act like
i just don't understand, but i can't,
because i kno with all the spiritual clarity i'm capable of,
that u did yr work.
& that's why u're in the top 20 of my league of extradinary blk men.
the ultimate brother, the kind i wish my own bros had grown
    up to be.
a walking-talking nguzo saba, u lived at the highest level of
    each principle, everyday & twice during kwanzaa.
in guarding the sanctity of our unity, u've been a warrior supreme
a one-man anti-defamation league, rescuing our images, again &
    again from blk trash marketers. the straightness of yr walk
has been a knife in the back of our enemies.
the crowned prince of collaboration, u've jammed with every-
    one who cld be played with, and extended yrself to every blk
    group committed
to restoring our people to their traditional pomp and splendor.
yr consistency has been the glue that seals our togetherness.
loyal to the finest degree, what others readily pimped u have
    notably protected. yr combined talents, & strengths have
    been a feast used only to satisfy our cultural hunger. in the
    daily tick-tock of yr life, u've been the mirror of our identity,
    a living shrine to our divine purpose, a perfectly directed
    arrow towards our liberation.

no matter how history treats yr biography,
u've got the warrior queen's seal of approval from me.

LAINI MATAKA

tsunami
blues (sri lanka, 2005)

In an awesome display of what she'll do to cleanse herself
mother nature let loose. hundreds of thousands
were extricated with no regard to rank & serial #
immediately the world checked its coffers
and the first figure the u.s. came up with,
was $35,000,000.

35 mil
the combined nickels & quarters amerikans
found in their couches last year.
35 mil
the salary of three NBA players for one season's work
that doesn't even lead to the play-offs.
35 mil
the current rate of exchange for thirty pieces of silver
dating back to the crucifixion.
35 mil
the fortuitous lottery winnings on a dollar.
35 mil
less than the absurd cost georgie jr. spent on his coronation.
35 mil
one day's box-office receipts for "the day after".
35 mil
dogs in amerika spend that & double on their food,
not to mention their clothes.
35 mil
the combined annual costs of Cosby's cigars, Oprah's diets,
Usher's dance lessons and Janet's makeovers.
35 mil
the numerical equivalent of contempt
as calculated & proposed by the world's most contemptuous.

keepin
it real!

u claim u wanna be loved, well
arent u at least engaged
in loving yrself?
u say u're tired of cooking for one, but
if yr solitude threatened to walk out today
wld u go chasing after?
u contend that u want yr life to have
greater meaning, but
if the reason for yr existence
shows up today
wld u try to break.
u scream u're disgusted with racism, but
if racism was dragged off to the gas-chamber today
sure u wldnt try to get a stay of execution?
u keep sing-songing about wanting the truth
but if the truth kissed u good-morning
wld u kick it out of bed?
u chant about being on the path
but if the path blisters rockier than
where u are now, will u
retreat into stagnation?

u swear yr life needs more meaning
but if reality turned into a window for u to truly see
wld u start backing down under a cadre of 'isms,
or wld u stand & flagrantly deliver?
u say u want more God in yr life
but if God appeared in yr mirror
cld u stand to embrace
yr true identity?

LAINI MATAKA

can wite-people
celebrate kwanzaa?

sure.
to honor the day of UMOJA
they can unwrap their secret scrolls, & review how much
time, energy and money they've spent destroying our unity.
to mark the day of KUJICHAGULIA
they can dress up in ivory robes, & reenact
how they strategically butchered our self-determination
with the persecution of those who spoke up for us.
on behalf of the day of UJIMA
they can pull out their sacred whips & relive
the glorious days of old, when they had us fully employed;
& their children were tutored in the womb
on the necessity of ripping the life outa
any signs of our working together.
in deference to the day of UJAMAA
they can extol the shrewdness of desegregation,
& how it bamboozled us into a double-edged freedom, while our
collective economics crawled from practice to theory.
out of respect for the day of NIA
they can praise with dollar bills & dirty condoms
their deity, the almighty media
for its role in destroying
and crippling the multi-purposes for our being.
in celebration of the day of KUUMBA
they can toast the demonic creativity that has
enabled them to send us flying back to our Creator
in horrid numbers,
while those of us who still process breath
withdraw deeper into denial.

THE PRINCE OF KOKOMO

to commemorate the day of IMANI
they can light candles to the system of wite supremacy that
their ancestors sired/& that they, with blood, piss & lies
have kept dutifully in tact, while terrorizing our every semblance
of faith.

OF COURSE,
wite people can celebrate kwanzaa;
as soon as they complete their 400 year initiation.

the invasion of
the hoochie-mamas

1.

since i'm seein more of it than i can bear
i looked up the word to try to understand
& cleavage means to split, didnt say nothin
bout titties.
which takes me right back to where i started from
why are those exotic mounds in my face?
if u're not about to breast-feed a child
why are yr breasts bidding everyone welcome?
since they're on exhibit
are they for everybody or
did u have someone special in mind,
& wldju kno him if u saw him?
if they're not to be sampled like chocolates
in an open box, then why are they sitting
up in their cups sayin bite me?

2.

can u buy me something, after all i did letchu smell it
can u help me out wif my phone bill, after all i did letchu feel it
can u help me wif some groceries, after all, i did letchu taste it
can u help me wif my rent, after all, i did letchu spend the night
unsuspecting buyers, beware,
before u plunge into seminal bliss,
go over her body with a microscope
cuz some where u least expect
there might be a price-tag.

3.

with more fiber in her hair than her diet
she flipped her simulated tresses in place
& with her eye-brows arched to the top of her forehead

THE PRINCE OF KOKOMO

her fox fur, truth hiding lashes
her 'i can blow u better than she can' lipstick
her sprayed on, see-through, back-out blouse
her now u see it, now u dont skirt
her casually sexed up pumps with matching hump-me bag,
she let the mirror have one more glance
as she wriggled her skirt down to where it cldnt stay.
locking reason inside, she stepped onto the corridor
where hundreds of her kind,
splashed multi-colored feathers, as they preened & paced
waiting for midnight to signal
the quest for unclaimed meat
on U st.

LAINI MATAKA

cousin walter

luvs powders
as long as they're white with a bite
will steal
to keep the queens in his veins
on their death-dealing thrones.

knows jail
better than he knows his own body
is married to a low-lifed heroin/e
who spends his vitality like chump change
still,
he wont snatch a blkwoman's purse
not even to neutralize cold turkey.

has been committing suicide
for a quarter of a century, but the only
thing that dies are the people he luvs.
to his children, he is an entity
they've all found alternatives for.
no one is tuned into him, or the fact
that one night, he broke thru his own high
to stop the rape
of a woman he didnt even kno.

after all
the multiple heart-aches his addiction
caused his motha/after all
the times he violated othas,
cousin walter threw his junkie self up against
the maniacal viciousness of a rapist
& redeemed himself for at least
two thousand seasons.

THE PRINCE OF KOKOMO

the good book

there is no book LARGE enuff
to contain all truths
and no human discernible enuff
to recognize them.
any book that leads u to yr god-self is holy
any book that points to the divine
as something otha than u
is propaganda
& was probably written by men
still angry about having to settle for penises.

there is no book so HOLY
that it includes ALL the ways there are
to interpret or access Spirit.
and the reason no such book exists, is becuz
God knows, most of the world's people
can't read.
what all-powerful, all-loving deity
wld create such a body of knowledge
then hide it from her/his children
& watch them suffer?

LAINI MATAKA

one of a million grievances
concerning yr death

(FOR WILL GREEN)

not one dance to remember
accidentally or deliberately forget;
no two-step or basement grind to reflect
where our bodies cld like hands in prayer
join the primordial sway
of all the lovers before us, who
beheld each otha just once: and knew.

for the dismissed, but unforgotten arguments,
tears, and the concomitant pain
that evolved simultaneously with the
tumultuous joy of luvin u: i have no regrets.
i just wish we'd had that first or last dance
to press gently between the pages of our loverhood.

if we'd had one two-step, one leg-entwined drag
i cld, on a dysfunctional night like this,
press the holographic button on my emotional body
& have u here right now, sweatin lightly,
leanin into me on a 45 degree angle,
whisperin my name, and wantin to kno,
if anybody's home at my house.

THE PRINCE OF KOKOMO

now that u're dead

now that u're dead, u choose me
is that how it goes? now
that there's nothing to lose, no risk
involved, i'm the one.
now that u can touch me w/out
parental reprisals,
lies are superfluous.
finally i am within yr price range.
u can afford to be all over me, inside of me
through me, anytime u want, confident
as a guardian of my spirit
that i will never reject u…
well, come on then.

LAINI MATAKA

welfare
reform

every time the sun rises
the u.s. gives israel
millions of dollars for nothing!
generations since 1947
have become dependent upon
those welfare checks.
they in turn
spy on the u.s. govt & its allies
& on various occasions they've
offered their butt to be kissed
while energizing a war of attrition
against the palestinian people.

if the bush administration
wants to reform the nation's welfare policy
why dont they treat israel like poor black people
& just cut'em off;
give them the opportunity to be self-sufficient.
put them in low-level programs that will train them
to work at mcdonald's, build their own homes
instead of trying to claim the ones their families abandoned
hundreds and hundreds of years ago.

if they'd drop israel from their welfare roles
maybe they'd have enuff money to
offer quality health care to their own citizens
like cuba does.

THE PRINCE OF KOKOMO

no one steals
my joy

(FOR KIBWE BEY)

no gradations of darkness
can taint my awareness of the sun;
no series of events
can nullify the miracle of my being Alive;
no vignettes of hell
can colonize the serenity of my now;
no sorrows remembered
can stand up to the immensity of my joy;
no promise of tomorrow
can tempt a trade-in on my today;
no amount of riches
can pry me away from the glory of this moment;
no proximity to death
can diminish the rapture of this second;
nothing man can conspire to do
or bring into existence,
can alter or stifle the mighty flow
of God reigning supreme in my soul.

LAINI MATAKA

post traumatic
slavery disorder

lettie and tom
had just finished jumpin the broom
when massah jake kicked in the door
pushed tom to the floor
raped lettie
and dared them to speak on it.
three incarnations later
tom looks at lettie
douses her with memory
and sets her on fire.

mad math
and thensome...

one moment
of white
privilege,
is worth
ten years
of opportunity
in
the lives
of
a hundred black people.

LAINI MATAKA

easy
does it

(FOR WALTER MOSLEY)

in case u
was thinkin
bout killin Mouse
u remember that movie called Misery
donchu?

psychology 101

compensation: when u cant do something well, u turn around and do something else.
wite - when u cant play ball, u become a sports announcer.
black - when u dont make the nba, u become a drug dealer.

daydreaming: is a simple form of escape from unpleasant facts or situations.
wite - u are disappointed in yr lack of melanin, rather than seek the ultimate solution, u daydream about being the most beautiful species in some made up jungle.
black - u cant deal with the reality of bein blk in a racist world, so u dye yr hair blonde.

displacement: is transferring what u feel from its original source to another object.
wite - u are angry with nature for not giving u more color, so u kill as many people of color as possible.
black - u are angry with wite people for oppressing u, so u also kill as many people of color as possible.

idealization: is placing exaggerated value on someone or something.
wite - giving the 2000 academy award to kevin spacey instead of denzel washington .
black - is claiming wite women treat blk men better than blk women do. or that the wite man treats his woman better than the blk man does.

identification: happens when u assume the qualities of

psychology 101 *(continued)*

someone u admire.

wite - i am wite with dreadlocks, i am a wite rapper, i play wite jazz , while i eat wite chocolate.

black - i have good hair, my grandmother was mixed, black people dont need no reparations.

projection: is blaming someone else for yr actions or thoughts.

wite - we captured/& sold blk people into slavery because they had no souls.

black - is pointing to wite people as the sole reason we suffer.

rationalization: offering acceptable reasons for yr behavior, though they're not the real reasons.

wite - u want to be rich, but u dont want to work for it, so u enslave people to work for u and claim its in the bible.

black - is saying u have to sell drugs because u cant find a job.

reaction formation: is behavior that shows opposite habits of those u truly possess.

wite – having stolen the native amerikans' land, u then insult them by declaring november as the month when they can show their faces.

black - u 're the descendents of the first people to use language, and u act like u cant read.

regression: is reverting to the behavior of a child.

wite - is threatening afrikan nations by withholding food if they dont vote yr way in the UN.

black - is walkin around with yr pants hangin down, while the

wealth of the world is being redistributed among the same
people who had it before.

repression: is trying to bury conscious thoughts in the uncon-
scious part of the mind.
wite - u've wiped out whole species of animals and people but
dont remember a thing about it.
black - u've been raped, drowned, disemboweled, enslaved,
castrated, and u dont remember a thing about it.

sublimation: is channeling unacceptable impulses into
socially acceptable goals.
wite - u dont want people of color to out-number u, and u cant
kill them all, so u discover cloning.
black - u wish u cld give wite people what they really and truly
deserve, instead, u watch oprah.

substitution: is replacing one goal for another attainable goal.
wite - u dont kno how to be one with the earth, so u destroy it.
black - u cant dismantle wite supremacy so u join the **naacp.**

communion

Cortez told the Aztecs
They must give up their idols
& abstain from human sacrifices
instead, they must
drink the blood of Christ
& eat the flesh of Jesus.

the prince of kokomo

(MY BROTHER STEVEN ROBINSON)

my brother the prince
was spun out of the desires of freedom run amok;
pitch black darker than a thousand Oswego nights
with a fineness known only to jet porcelain;
son of a hoodoo whispering priest,
the same mold shaped them tho
different times birthed them.

my brother the prince,
native to a tribe of men
too magnetic for their own good
(or anybody else's)
handled his spear in the family tradition
piercing first/inquiring never.

my brother the prince
was more brilliant than ten inner-harbor sunsets,
more awesome than a dawn painting itself over Druid Hill
    Park,
more electric than Cherry Hill after dark.
on his worse day, in every way he was still
Kokomo fine, straight outa Ethiopia fine, what no tanning
spa can offer fine, should've had his own empire fine,
looked stunning in white fine.

my brother the prince
loved to feel the wind in his face as he sprinted through
time & space/he was so fast!
cldve been jesse fast,
wld try anything once fast, cldnt help but catch a fire fast.
he was grease lightning---so high-speed

LAINI MATAKA

the prince
of kokomo (continued)

he outran love, stayed miles ahead of marriage
and left friendship in the dust.

my brother the prince
was a play august wilson shld have written.
a shining blu/blk who questioned the crown on his head;
an aristocrat with a penchant for illicit pipe dreams
which he wrestled with until he ran out of breath
and there was nothing left but the afterglow of his fineness,
the last sigh of his vitality and the blue echoes
of parental whispers pulling at him from that 'better place'.

cant shoot the
breeze w/out trees

(FOR JULIA BUTTERFLY MILLS)

she only shinnied up there to make a point.
she was the first one surprised, when it turned
into months. wonder if she lost herself,
turned tree. turned sister to the bark
started wearing it like a skin graft.
her english realizing its arrogance
started deferring to the sounds coming up
from the redwoods roots.
the guttural cry of something that has outlived
every thing in its vicinity.
its eminence roars out its desire to live
& manifests in the form of a white butterfly,
living out in human flesh meshed in a giant tree
an appendage of nature, a thousand years old.

who cld un-muzzle the teeth that wld chew
a millennium of existence away
to land on a Japanese table as chop-sticks
or the main pillar in the home for the rich & famous.

that someone shld have to jeopardize life & limb
to protest the intended murder of nature's archives
successfully demonstrates how
when people come upon something in a vile way
they never fully value it.
their forefathers butchered millions of animals and humans
to get their paws on this land, now they kill the land.
why dont they kill themselves, then maybe everything else can live.

LAINI MATAKA

cant shoot the breeze
w/out trees *(continued)*

just one of those trees is more informed
than all of its human contemporaries.
we do not exist for trees, anymore than they exist for us.
we are both rooted to the hot, wet and dark of life
that the earth has been charitable enuff to grant us by
fastening us both to the circular ends of breathing.
yet some slobbering fool, draws deeply on that breath
then sends out a crew to destroy the source.
some idiot, with monetary cataracts on his eyes
tries to impersonate God
by giving the order to fell the redwood of giants
that have been on this earth for a thousand summers;
witnessed a millennium of environmental changes, and bur-
    geoned
into a vital facet of this hemisphere's true allure.

maybe we shld all adopt a tree
before we allow another one of nature's fingers to be cut off
we shld all be laying our bodies down around that precious forest,
as if it were a storage place for our future breaths.
we shld go to war with anyone who tries to
to chainsaw our mother's children
for some nickel & dime bullshit
that the original land-holders
wld never have tolerated or deigned to imagine.

somewhere in the mythical middle east

(INSPIRED BY MARVIN X)

arabian blood has never claimed me
and hebrew leaves me dumbfounded;
the bible neglected to mention my father by name,
and canaan was not a section in my neighborhood;
but I wld fight to the death
if someone tried to evict me from my domain
& relegate me to some raggedy hovel on the edge of nowhere.
i wld throw down with any means at my disposal
if some fool sd to me,
"u've gotta give up yr home, cause my family
pissed on that soil thousands of years ago".

nuclear weapons cld not stop me
from clinging to my abode;
hanker-chief heads cldnt affect me
ak-47's wld not deter me
& anthrax wld only spur me.

he who is often mistaken for human
cannot bulldoze the dreams of another w/out repercussions.
thieves have no right to sunny skies,
& good times are prohibited for those who kill
on behalf of fables or steal another's birthright
to validate tales told by an idiot.
wail yr balls off at the wall of waiting,
gentrify judea and samaria all u want
just kno that karma has her eyes on u
& none of yr bombs will be smart enuff
to keep her at bay.

.

LAINI MATAKA

inside pocket

Most of us have an inside pocket full of stuff
we need to throw away,
stuff we've been collecting since childhood;
stuff we can whip out 20 years later &
shut somebody up with;
stuff we can one day resurrect & end a
relationship with.

Most of us have an inside pocket
full of stuff we need to get rid of as soon as
we finish reading this pome.
stuff we've been holding against our parents & siblings,
stuff we've been holding against life &
sometimes God;
stuff that gets uglier & smellier
the longer we hold on to it.

Most of us have an inside pocket full of memories
we're not even sure really happened;
stuff we hold onto till it fuses into the muscle & cartilage
of our being.
some of us wld rather die/than relinquish
just a lil bit of all that stuff,
becuz letting go means change,
& change means growth,
& growth means learning to
embrace bliss & torment
with the same passion.

THE PRINCE OF KOKOMO

about my
sistah freda

my sistah was bewitched by poppies;
often exchanged her beauty for theirs
always got the worse part of the deal.
like the poppy
she was cut down, processed into
a frightening substance
specifically employed to defile
souls on ice.

used into gauntness,
her failing immune system
retired to the family attic
dying finally, to the relief of herself,
her guardian spirits
and the united states govt.

LAINI MATAKA

and the
oscar goes to:

the academy awards shld give satan
a lifetime achievement award
for faking his own existence
& tricking millions into believing
that GOD cld have a credible rival.

ancient rumor

to empower the sight
with all its might
darkness is
the sincerest form of light

LAINI MATAKA

there's paralysis in
our analysis

since amerika is wite supremacy's most zealous devotee
and elections are its way of allowing its pawns
to think they can move about freely on the chessboard.
when we pull those levers, what do we expect to happen?
that unemployment will cease, that we'll get one of the
50 acres and a fifth of mule? that all the guns will high-tail it
outa our communities, dragging crack along behind them?
when we pull those levers/do we think we're blks having an
amerikan experience? & when we find out our candidate won,
does that mean wite people will stop being so wite?

we cling to voting like its our greatest & only chance
to invoke change; our one and only lifeboat.
we misrepresent ancestors & claim we must
participate in the process becuz of their past suffering,
while ignoring the fact that their analysis
was rooted in their times. since then, we've been
brutally uprooted & though we can identify the hour,
we never seem to kno what time it is.
we swear voting is the answer, and when it doesn't work
we still think it's the answer, and when it's proven to us
that it doesn't work, we still think it's the answer with a birth defect.

we always vote within the parameters of white choices.
we dare not vote for a Cynthia Mckinney,
or even a candidate of our own, chosen by our own interests.
the ancestors who got their heads busted open,
didn't kno that anything the system gives us,
can always be taken from us. so they accepted

the right to vote even though it was stamped with an
    expiration date.
they told me to tell u, that they only believed in the vote
when it was accompanied by resistance on all other levels.
we're always choosing the lesser of two evils,
which is like sitting comfortably in manure
becuz it smells better than death.
voting at the polls is like casting a vote for wite people
voting is believing in their system;
voting is believing u are included in that system.
if u believe yr vote counts/u also think u matter to the system
and that one day wite people will slip up & be fair.

the people who raped us till we mutated, are the same people
who set up the electoral system, are the same people
who denied us participation in that system, are the same
people who lynched us with a smile, are the same
people who control the voting machines, are the same
people who now consider us non-essential, are the
same people who count the ballots, are the same people
who control the results, are the same people who're
customizing diseases to our dna, are the same people
who file our votes in the thrash, and claim our problem is
we don't turn out at the polls.

but as much as we huff and puff about the vote,
somehow our passion doesn't extend itself
to battling for the rights of those
who were sucked into the penal system
& stripped of their voting privileges/even tho they served
    their time.

LAINI MATAKA

there's paralysis in
our analysis *(continued)*

if voting is so, apropos, why don't I hear voices screaming
for justice till the glass is shattered
in every court house in this land.

if we've just gotta, gotta vote
why haven't we spent more energy
immunizing the voting process against the tricknology
we kno is forthcoming.
& if the whole voting piece is as sacred & holy as we intimate
then why doesn't it galvanize us all year long?
yes, the ancestors whose teeth were knocked out,
whose ribs were cracked, asked me to ask u,
when are u gonna honor their sacrifices by voting for yrself.
stop thinking the way things are is the only way they can be.
until we learn to vote for our own genius,
our own intelligence, our own natural gifts;
until we cast a ballot for our own autonomy,
our own power to alter reality;
until we elect ourselves to be the commander-in-chief of
our own fierceness & collective might,
we need to stay out of the polls
go find a manger, and wait for another miracle.

a warrant
issued by eros

i'm gonna stalk u like the IRS
hunt u down like a zealous karma
post yr mugshot all over the cosmos
& when i catch up with u,
i'm gonna happen all over u like
sun on the sahara.
i'm gonna luv the knots outa yr soul
& leave u feelin like a saint with his own holiday.
i'm gonna train yr senses to burst
with pleasure
at the very sound of my thighs
rubbing together when i walk.
no part of u will be neglected from the kinks
on yr scalp to the kinks around yr jewels.
matter of fact, i'm gonna macramé our
pubic hairs together/then work u up one
side of heaven and down the otha;
& if u havent turned neophyte by sunrise
i'm gonna use verbs on u that even yr dic-tionary
is afraid to define.
now, are u gonna cum quietly, or
is my tongue gonna havta use force.

LAINI MATAKA

obsessed with katrina tho we've never even met

fourteen days & a deluge of miseries later
bodies were still being found
trapped in deserted hospitals & abandoned jails
trapped in forsaken nursing homes, on roofs
in cars, in trees & floating pieces of whatever.
folks who wld never lay claim to a million dollar portfolio
were murdered by economically inspired neglect;
trapped in poverty & 3rd world bureaucracy;
trapped in the never ending exploitability of their skins;
with a sense of disbelief that only the innocent can radiate
they died trapped by wite gunslingers & the un-national guard,
they were drowned in smear campaigns
& strangled by the diabolical grip of gentrification.
blks three generations thick, died in their place of birth
trapped like refugees in the cobwebbed corners of their
own nation's nonchalance,
while their political overseers used their tax dollars
to stuff democracy down the unwilling throats of Iraqis.

2.
Cuba
a baby guerilla
breast-fed by the revolution
reared & honed by blk hands;
a bodacious speck on the map of human geography
made famous by amerika's maniacal disdain
& crippling embargos,
OFFERED
in spite of the actions against it
to send 1500 hurricane-trained doctors
to the hard hit residents of new orleans;
but the u.s. hates them so much

& cares about blk people so little,
that they refused/preferring the suffering of all those amerikans
over any assistance from a country that refuses
to gap its legs open for a red, white & blue reception.
but if the tragic figures had been yankees proper
the u.s. wldve stormed into Cuba like swartzeneggar
& kidnapped the country's medical staff
despite their willingness to come.

3.
Venezuela
courageous survivor of a u.s. backed coup,
OFFERED
in spite of cia efforts to kill its democracy
to send gallons of oil to help relieve the fake scarcity
blamed on katrina,
but the u.s., under the spiritual leadership
of the devil-worshipping pat robertson
wld rather see Chavez dead
than seek relief for it's own people.
but had the scarcity been real,
uncle sam wldve blown up Hugo
& drained the country
down to the last drop.

4.
England
home of mad dogs & scurrilous men
sent a hundred thousand UN approved meals
to the victims of katrina
but the u.s. claimed the food wasn't fit for human consumption
even tho it was finger-licking good enuff

LAINI MATAKA

obsessed with katrina tho we've never even met *(continued)*

for british & amerikan soldiers doing the shock & awe in Iraq.
& instead of sending it where it might stave off starvation
they put it aside for burning
becuz this is amerika/& we dont need help from
outsiders to feed insiders we've already marked for destruction.

5.
Spain
contributed foodstuffs/wasnt good enuff
Italy sent mega-groceries/wasnt good enuff
Israel sent gallons of pear juice/wasnt good enuff
before katrina, the u.s. didnt care
if the folks in new orleans were eating alligators
or if the alligators were eating them.
but once the rest of the world started weighing in
the FDA got up off its lazy ass,
threw together some standards,
& suddenly, the most foodstuffs, marked unfit for consumption
were donations earmarked for the victims of katrina.

6.
when the levees began to sag
like things ignored tend to do
& the frames buckled & strained like
cheney's bank accounts
a species of 'seals' alien to the gulf
were sent to put them out of their misery.

7.
blk folks are the leading experts in
memory lapses that extend over into centuries
of wanton, in yr face abuse,
a pattern of suffering must be embedded

in the nap of our hair.
cuz slavery wasn't really all that bad &
those good wite folks didn't quarantine us in the stupor dome
that wasn't blk us being passed over while the helicopters
stopped to pick up paleness.
those weren't dogs waving to us from air-conditioned buses
while we cried out in thirst.
we weren't really chest high in feces, blood & toxins
c'mon, no way that was us lining up to board those
destination unknown vehicles.
we weren't dumped into strange & hostile territories.
we didn't really let ourselves be separated from our children
& the guns in our faces didn't have nothing to do with why we
stopped trying to rescue each other.
those rescuers weren't shooting at us, they were
tryin to get our attention.
& so what, they didn't mean it when they called us refugees
& they were only joking when they questioned our right
    to return.
nope, nope, nahhhh
see, i don't care whatchu say
this aint got nothing to do with race.

8.
when the origins of mental depravity
are in question
sooner or later the mystery points toward
the source. behold
barbara bush,
the marie antoinette of our times
moving daintily about the stupor dome
"cake anyone?"

LAINI MATAKA

obsessed with katrina tho we've never even met *(continued)*

9.
we are still in the middle of our passage
only now, the drug is wearing off.
& even our most devoted handkerchief heads
must admit secretly if not aloud, that
if katrina's victims hadn't been so blk & blu
the navy & the coast guard wldve stopped the earth's rotation,
to airdrop life preservers & rubber rafts over the flooded areas;
& before hunger cld threaten one pale stomach,
the restaurants in the french quarter
instead of letting vast quantities of food rot, wldve
been stuffing meals into every lipless mouth they cld find.
but then, if they had been of european ancestry
the levees near their homes wld've been just as
formidable as the ones that guarded industry.
if the displaced hadnt been so blk & blu,
the uss bataan, which was just idling nearby
wldve been given orders to
unleash their 1,200 man crew on hunger & thirst
while using their helicopters to airlift the wounded
for treatment in their 600 bed, state of the freeking art hospital.
if the 9th ward hadnt been so blk & blu
homeland security wld be investigating,
how & why a barge was catapulted into the wall
of the industrial canal, causing the deaths of hundreds of
innocent beings whose only crime, was living on land
some wite men were drooling over.
if the traumatized hadnt been so blk & blu
when they were allowed by the pit-bull police, the guard
& the blackwater mercenaries, to finally return to their homes

their meager belongings wld not have been strewn all over
    the ground
& their apartments wld not have been occupied by strangers
looking at them with contempt & paying 3 times the original
    rent.
28,000 blue eyes & blonde heads
wld not be sub-existing in shelters,
a month after any disaster, anywhere in these united states
especially while 38,000 empty public housing units
sat around languishing.

if the blk folks hadnt been so eternally blu,
if the first nation's people hadnt been so
historically disadvantaged,
if the cajuns hadnt been such an embarrassment,
if the latinos hadnt been so mixed-blooded,
maybe their govt wld not
have cock-blocked their rescue.

10.
4 months have passed
& the good ole boys are pinning eviction notices
on property that aint even standing.
the govt has declared that the devastated who live in hotels
must now pay their own way or hit the streets.
those unwillingly dispersed across the country
were given five days to return home to recoup their lost lives
& for some wicked reason, the greyhound
known for making stops in towns with one street
suddenly cancelled its service to new orleans.

obsessed with katrina tho we've never even met *(continued)*

11.
congressional hearings on katrina
were full of
pasty-faced humpty-dumpties
sittin up on the wall
with visions of hanukah dancing in their heads
as they displayed more ardent concern
over the blk use of
the term concentration camp,
than the applied reality.
the sistahs testifying responded so vehemently
that congressman ofay
shlda got the message, but being terminally wite
it was impossible for him to let
those blk mouths speak for themselves,
so he tried to minimize their experience by pointing out
that no one was killed in gas chambers
& they asked in response,
if the demise of babies by water instead of gas
made them less dead.
for it's a fact that
people were vigorously extracted from their homes;
they were confined like animals for slaughter
whiteys with weapons kept them from crossing over into relief;
they were denied food and water
& the right to search for either;
they were forced by gunpoint onto to buses w/out destinations;
they were wrenched like their ancestors from their children
    & families
& sprinkled across the country like bread crumbs,
for birds of prey.

& for those who managed to hold on
there aint even a box of welfare cheese
cause the rats in charge ran off with the cheddar.

12.
two years have had the nerve to pass
& yet,
the homeless are still battling the elements
the displaced have been dissed & placed arbitrarily
into minutes that will never turn into hours.
families are still trying to reunite
while govt agencies obstruct the flow of pertinent information.
FEMA
continues to lie, cheat & steal, while condaleeza
continues to shop for shoes.
& the only real news is that the gov't
may be guilty of failing new orleans
but it didn't fail wite supremacy.

LAINI MATAKA

not only will the pot call the kettle black, it'll try to take its place on the stove

self-ordained prophets leave heaven
jump on the first thing emitting smoke
to come to hell, where
they rant & rave to the survivors of hell
about how hot it is!

self-proclaimed, polyester sages, leave heaven
to come to hell,
to teach us infidels about the properties of heat.
we who've only been consumed by flames all our lives,
they wanna preach to us about how we shld be handling
those flames, when they left heaven smoldering; left their loved
ones in the conflagration of yankee imperialism
masquerading as NIKE & KFC (hope the c stands for chicken)

self-contained prophets, leave heaven
to cop some of hell's benefits, while
outa the otha side of their mouths, they curse us
till their accents fade & their children
evolve rejecting the country/heaven they once knew
& refused to fight to develop, becuz they wanted
something ready-made
like hell.

THE PRINCE OF KOKOMO

father philip berrigan

u never can tell what camp
a soldier will emerge from
be it the catholic church
or the human heart.
it is within this context that
bloodying draft records
and disarming nukes
take on the definition
of bravery;
above the holy grail &
beyond the silent majority
non-violent duty called
till death pointed a respectful finger.

if heaven exists
there is no other where he cld possibly be
if not
he can come right back here to us;
unfortunately, we still need him.

LAINI MATAKA

cultural
impersonators

they look blk
sport locks that lie
& afrikan clothes made in korea.
when they're not humming "LIFT EVERY VOICE...
(dont kno the words)
they meet secretly with wite people
over what to do with otha colored people.
they think they're free in the accidental
color of their skins;
that the word gentrification secretly includes them.
back in the day, they always stayed,
while everybody else was running away.

they've got houses
full of afrikan art & minds full of uncle tom thoughts
superior in pimping even to iceberg slim
they exploit blk beauty as if their survival is contingent
upon accrued interest & empty-headed booty.
they rent and sell to whites what blacks
are dying for want of.
they brag about money to people they
kno have none
& are fool enuff to think they're actually liked
by someone.

they lip-sync tributes to the blk collective
while they cheat and abuse blk individuals;
always the first to show up at high profile blk functions
always the last to internalize the real sentiments.
always judging who's worthy enuff to save,
wldnt surprise me if their ancestors had slaves.

THE PRINCE OF KOKOMO

the cost
of going home

once i gave up EVERYTHING
to go to Mother Afrika
and here u come
breaking yr neck to get here
cutting yr own umbilical chord,
surrendering an autonomy
(i wld have died for)
to meet the great enslavers.
the total of all yr experiences here
will never transform the complexities
of being born black in amerika
into something u can
comprehend and decode
to the roots back home.

LAINI MATAKA

love letters
to my liege

June 1, 2006

Dear Ancestors:

For most of my adult life, I've revered you and tried to give you
the daily tribute that you deserve. The more greatness I
discovered in our history, the more I prostrated myself before
you. When I calculated the sum total of your worth, I found
myself to be the final equation. The more I appreciated you,
the more space you began to occupy in my being. The inner
voice that has been my life's guide, is now indistinguishable
from yours. No matter where I go, I feel I'm surrounded by
an entire entourage; a magnet for blessings that can't wait to
catch up with me. And I'm grateful.

Signed,

Yr servant

June 2nd

Dear Ancestors;

I've been representing you for quite a while now. Like a dutiful
wife to her husband, when you knock on my door I always
open it. When I try to recite a poem, and you take over my
mouth, I never complain. And yet, those things I require
to maintain some kind of balance in my life, I'm still
w/out. How can this be so, if everyday, I sing to you. Pour
my voice like water into libations for you. Call your names
with all the sacredness of the medu netcher. There's more
food on your altar than there is in my refrigerator. And yet
the sound of tiny feet have never filled my home. Space is the
name of the face that greets my every morning. And the work
you've ordained me to do, raises and restores the wretched/

while ignoring the rent that's due. I can't even sleep thru
the night, for taking dictation from you; which I continue
to do, even tho my needs look like a soup kitchen line back
in 1942. Can't something in this life be just for me?
Signed,
Frustrated

June 3rd
Dear Ancestors:
In an effort to seal the spaces between us, to better
          comprehend our relationship, I mailed out a sample
          of myself to several indigenous religions, and they very
          lovingly, mailed me right back. They said destroying wite
          supremacy was my religion, my soul the no. #1 temple,
          and my heart, the only priestess. And I can appreciate
          that, but where do you come in? In the past, I've loved the
          idea of Afrika so much, that I thought ancestors cld never
          be talked about or thought of in anyway that was not holy.
          But struggling to keep my covenant with you, w/out the
          basic things that my heart & soul require, has made me
          question our relationship. Who are you, if not the people
          that have gone on before? Human beings who left this
          plane taking with you the whole range of human
          emotions. How foolish of me to think, that death
          automatically transforms a selfish, irresponsible person,
          into a generous and loving ancestor. How did I ever
          expect, a person who denied their africanity all through
          life, to suddenly cross over into a spirit of consciousness?
          I've decided, that ours is a partnership and not a

LAINI MATAKA

love letters
to my liege *(continued)*

dictatorship. I am not here for you to ride into the
ground as reparations for the lives you were denied.
As long as I honor and build upon yr memory, I expect you
to honor and assist my existence.
Signed,
Yr partner

June 4th
Dear Ancestors:
Are we having a failure to communicate here? My job hasn't
   paid me in two months, my suit case is dragging in court and
   I'm entering my tenth year of abstinence. Yet I call yr names
   everyday, remind those around me to do the same, and share
   yr significance every chance I get. Could it be, you can't
   make out what I'm saying, because the proper rituals were
   never done to open yr ears? No words were ever uttered to
   ancestralize you, to mark yr place in eternity, to make you
   aware of the awesomeness of yr human-plus powers. Is the
   fact that I call yr names generically, the reason the assistance
   I receive is generic as well?. Maybe I need to be more specific.
   When my pockets are thin, I need to call on my Dad who
   cld whip a dollar out of reality's every dimension. When my
   enemies surround me, I need to call my five-foot Aunt Nez,
   who fought everybody from her 6'3" husband, to Baltimore
   City's finest police. Maybe if I customize my prayers, you'll
   maximize yr response.
Signed
Yr evolving partner

June 5th

Dear Ancestors:

I keep trying to contact various ones of you, but only one of you
ever seems to show. Is that how y'all flow? Do I use his soul
as the scroll to write my messages upon? Do I focus on him
like he focuses on me, and trust that he delivers the word to
the rest of you? Appeals made solely on the basis of shared
blood, can emancipate and empower those of you who
mean no good, because no good was the only card you ever
drew from life's deck. I must be more specific; invite only
the righteous to swim in the purity of my soul. Use words
like bars to fend off the ones with evil intent. Just as there
is no room in my life for people who refuse to walk
THE GREAT BLK WAY, there is no room in my spirit for
ancestors who won't illuminate it.

Signed

Getting clearer all the time.

June 6th

Dear ancestors:

This is the worst shape we've been in since the coming of the
ships & I'm told you're under-employed; that we don't use
you enough. That you're just mulling around in the mist,
waiting for us to declare our needs. But how can this be,
when so many of us are calling you like crazy? Walking
around in the street pleading with you under our breath.
How many voices do we have to recruit just to put a dent
in our oppression? How many prayers must we combine
to keep death from stealing our heroes? What rituals can

love letters
to my liege *(continued)*

we enact to stop fear from gripping our hearts? How many
petitions must we sign in blood, before a reversal of fortune,
propels us into a black victory? And how much of our
collective weight, is really mine to carry?
Signed
Really need to know

June 7th
Dear Ancestors:
In the last few weeks we've lost, Damu Smith, Jackie McClean,
   Nestor Hernandez, Rufus Houston, Dr. Prem Deben, John
   Hicks, Hylton Ruiz and Billy Preston. What the heck
   is going on?
Signed
Holla if you hear me.

those who share a stomach, cant afford to be enemies

a chained, two-headed dog
digs around in the yard
looking for sustenance.
the hand that chains them
throws them one bone,
they tear each otha apart
tryin to claim the bone.
they shlda tore up the hand,
split the bone
& jumped the fence.

LAINI MATAKA

the queen of
spades

easily, the grand diva of modern world politics
she's also one of the most duplicitous.
unanimously, the most strategically laid up
black person on the planet
she's also one of the most mentacidal.
indubitably, one of the top three mouths
able to access the emperor's ear,
voted most likely to succeed
as a corporate consort.

hailing from Bombingham, Alabama
she mushroomed in a home where Martin Luther King
was vehemently opposed
becuz he wanted too much too soon.
she knew two of the unforgettable four
obliterated on that day, & w/out giving the
slightest tell-tale sign of physical injury or trauma
she very quietly shed her core, dismissed her blood
& started 'passing'.

razor-like even then in her powers of discernment
she knew the meek wld never see one acre of their inheritance,
so she swore like scarlet o'hara never to be poor,
never to be poorly situated, and never to give five
on the black hand side. she closed the inner doors of fate
& vowed never to emulate or associate with those
whose children were so easy to violate.

she spent her youth auditioning for the Stockholm Syndrome
(which wasnt even recruiting)
reactionary to the bone, she uncapped her brilliance

letting it pour freely into vessels, always alien to her own.
her mind was laundered like dirty money,
at amerika's finest institutions of higher earning.
with her ph.d., she picked the lock on chevron's doors,
& proved to be just as mercenary as the big dogs.
accepting her share of fleas & securities, she took a vow of
silence & watched in self-negating complicity,
as chevron slithered into the Niger Delta,
where it bombarded the air
with toxic filth & slowly putrefied the waters, that devastated the
crops which poisoned the people who were forced to breathe
in that toxic filth & bathe their babies in those putrefied waters.
years later when the mothers of those babies realized that chevron
was the culprit, that chevron was intimately tied to their
child's listlessness, the plethora of pains being born w/out names,
the fevers their herbs cldnt recognize.;
they locked arms & marched on chevron
causing a temporary shut-down.

by then, the queen had already made her bones & was ripe for
papa doc's anointing. & he bestowed upon her,
new chest hair & a deeper voice, which she never once used
to free any black people or women anywhere.
by the time the u.s. had trained Afrikan men in how to
use their self-loathing, to beat down the women to protect
        chevron,
she had graduated to the esteemed rank
of baby doc's right-hand man.
& no matter how grossly he farted,
she was always prepared to push him aside & claim the stink.

LAINI MATAKA

the queen of
spades *(continued)*

second only to colonic powell, they both deserve oscars
for acting like blacks run something in amerika.
which automatically qualifies them as co-killers
in any & all amerikan interventions around the globe.
& the exemptions that many countries & insurgents
have traditionally granted blacks from random acts of terrorism
are no longer applicable.

past loyalties cast her as the only skirt in the bush-whack gang,
which pushed her out on the stage to guarantee the world,
not her family, but the world, not just black people,
but the world, not just amerikans, but the world,
that Iraq had weapons of mass destruction which would sooner
or later be aimed at the u.s.
she pleaded her case like Johnnie Cochran
& babies got blown up (just like the unforgettable four.
tens of thousands of Iraqis were blasted into oblivion
by u.s. made depleted uranium-tipped missiles.
& tho she was just a surrogate bomber with an ugly hairdo,
her finger was powerful enuff to do the pointing.
she who had survived the bombings of people blk & poor,
was finally in a position, sick enuff & high enuff
to bomb somebody else.

& now that it's clear even to Stevie Wonder,
that mendacity has been riding her tongue
& the only weapons found have been those of mass distortion,
not once has she apologized to the nation or to the Iraqi people;
which implies, that she's unremorseful about the bourgeoning
cemeteries, hardly concerned about the truncated survivors,
    feels no

THE PRINCE OF KOKOMO

sense of responsibility for all the bloody booty,
aint lost one night of sleep
over those whose new address is yesterday;
& probably dashes off to eat a rare steak,
every time Iraqis & hunger are mentioned in the same sentence.
at best, she probably lights a candle
on behalf of all the innocent people who God has not
blessed to be amerikans. black ice in overdrive
she processes the deaths of amerikan soldiers
for about as long as it takes to brush her teeth.
i wonder if she haunts the halls of Walter Reed,
taking the edge off her conscience
with genetically engineered smiles and treats
for those who ran off to serve their country
but came back with star-spangled stumps for legs.

winner of the fabricator of the year award
at the confirmation hearings/she has finally
reached her greatest pinnacle;
pro-Israeli to the point of thinking Ashkenazi,
staunch supporter of bending the free world
into a Dred Scott position,
gold-medal winner in the violation of others' human rights
she picks her teeth with the bones of little Omars & Kadijahs
notice the close reptilian eyes,
as they slowly turn towards Iran & Syria.
may God save us all from the executive skeezer
the black medusa, condelezza.

LAINI MATAKA

who
'dat'

(FOR AMIRI BARAKA)

who beat the hell outa english
sent it screaming & wailing back to the manor born.
who wrote, "everything u ever wanted to kno,
about blacks, but were too white to ask";
who sounds like miles on paper,
who had his own house of congress before
the caucus even knew they were blk.
who like a pit-bull when he gets his teeth
into a piece of truth.
who gives blood transfusions to anemic poets;
who loves the journey so much, forgets
to get paid for being an agent.
who so scholarly
he gonna havta die & come back again just
to answer his own questions.
who has lived so thoroughly for the people
who've lived so half-ass for him.
who pays with his life-force for the
accuracy of his words.
who fillets the truth & bares it open
for even the blind to see.
who is too tall to fit in most libraries.
who shld we let kiss our babies foreheads.
who is the Father of scribes, the Mansa of metaphors
the Zorro of similes.
who else can boast of reaching elder-hood
w/out a hint of betrayal.
who? who? who?

loose barrels make the most money

Cedric, who
wish he was an entertainer
cracked
on Rosa Parks, who
with the simple stationing of her royal behinds,
caused more history to unfurl
than his barbershop mentality
will ever absorb.

LAINI MATAKA

the duality
of terrorism

thousands of relatively innocent people/daddies,
mommies, aunties
grandpa's, immersed in a.m. rituals, just going about
their business,
wondering what they'd have for lunch, maybe, or whether they
cld finally close that deal. they all opened their eyes that
morning, expecting to be alive that night.

millions of us were just living our lives;
on our way to a
neighboring village, coming from a shrine, maybe goin
to see Nana
or looking for wood to make a drum; some of us didnt even
have to leave home,
cuz the WHITE PLAGUE stomped right into our sacred space.
none of us had risen that day with the faintest vision of what
wld occur before night.

of the thousands gathered, some had shown up with hang-overs,
headaches, cramps. some were weighted down by events
of the day before,
some hadnt even had their first cup of coffee yet. some
had arrived bristling
with the energy necessary to manipulate high finances.
some walked about
with xerox'd smiles, wishing to God they'd taken a
mental health day.

millions of us were caught creating, mating, praying;
some of us were

THE PRINCE OF KOKOMO

readying for the first hunt, some were preparing for circumcision.
some were right in the middle of "tribal" councils
sure to affect the welfare of thousands of people;
& the WHITE PLAGUE swept right thru with gunpowder
& diseased intentions/turning spears into toothpicks,
& ebony skins into a bastard economy.
when they got hit, nothing they had ever experienced,
cld offer them any clues.
death & destruction was right upon them & their minds did all
all kinds of flip flops, trying to understand.
the blood in their veins was saturated with adrenalin.
impossible acts of bravery clamored to be done,
with only God to bear witness.
& for those who substituted self-control for
spirit, their misplaced faith was ostentatiously
snatched away/causing them to lose
their minds before it was even certain they'd lose their lives.

initially, when the WHITE PLAGUE hit, we thought the world
was coming to an end. whole villages full of people were
corralled, roped & branded;
we screamed for our gods till our tongues fell out, & the
PLAGUE raged on
blind to all aspects of human decency, deaf to all wailings
including God's.
& there were no herbs or spells to fight it becuz it was
alien & self-perpetuating.
& even though some of us made it
from one shore to the other/our humanity was ripped to shreds.
the conflagration huffed & puffed like a mighty ogre,

LAINI MATAKA

the duality
of terrorism *(continued)*

determined to devour everything in its sight.
people leapt to instant death, rather then feed the ogre's
profane appetite.
othas were never allowed a choice/and they returned to their Maker
angry, confused & unprepared to accept their place in the after-life.

as untold millions squeezed thru the middle passage,
those whose legs werent too abused to walk, who had the
fortitude of mind
to keep the WHITE PLAGUE from invading their last inner-recesses,
waited endlessly for one fortuitous moment, when the
chains wld relax
& they cld leap to honorable death by shark or sea.

and of the thousands who the flames cldnt find instantly,
tons of steel & stone became their tombstones.
time ceased to be segmented, as they lay lodged like mortar
between bricks
not knowing what wld happen next.
they held on with ethereal claws to the lives they'd led before that day.
embracing their pain with gigantic question marks: what
had they done?
& even if God was inclined to answer, they wanted life too
desperately to listen.

for us who totaled millions, time stretched like leather into
hundreds of years of not knowing what wld happen next.
who knew while iron
kept our wrists & ankles in its jaws, that never again
wld there be seasons, rites of passage, or any need to separate time

THE PRINCE OF KOKOMO

becuz under the WHITE PLAGUE all time wld be the
same: brutal.
& for us there wld be no rescuers, no merciful death
by avalanche or suffocation.

many of the missing thousands, died calling their mothers
or praying for sweet life for their children.
some gave themselves to Spirit, understanding for the first
time, who was really in charge.
some fought to the end, refusing to give up
the abundant lives they'd been living. they all died traumatized
by the absurdity
of why this was happening to them.
most of them ruled out karma, some never
even considered it, even tho it's karma that ultimately signs
all of our obituaries.

too many of us millions died thanking God for delivering us
from the WHITE PLAGUE.
we didnt even care how death came as long as it cld force open
the putrid jaws of the PLAGUE, long enuff to pull us out of it.
the rest of us died all day, everyday, wondering why the people
we were stolen from never came after us.
we died every night the PLAGUE flared up in our loins like VD,
or left bloody tracks down our backs.
we died trying to peel off our skin,
since it seemed to be the thing that made us so susceptible
to ruin.
we died w/out being counted & often w/out being identified.

LAINI MATAKA

the duality
of terrorism *(continued)*

the thousands were lauded & applauded. adorned & mourned.
no matter how many times they tried to stay dead,
the media wld dig them back up, & parade them around
on the screen.
no longer able to speak for themselves, their voices were
projected tirelessly
by everyone seeking a quick buck or a quick war.
funds that were unavailable for the nation's poor
came gushing through a sudden crack in the universe.
& though the deaths were catastrophic, causing
immeasurable pain & heartache;
their monetary value was quickly calculated.
thousands of families now stand to receive millions,
becuz they were devastated & disproportionably white.

& even though millions of us have survived, between the twin
towers of amerikan slavery & institutionalized racism, still,
millions more of us line the ocean's floor like a skeletal arrow
pointing towards the perpetrator.
where is our monument? our six-month, sixth century
anniversary?
our parade, our memorial, our acknowledgement?
as valiantly unforgettable as most of the 911 people were,
they were never forced to carry this nation on their backs,
& if being amerikans makes their families eligible for millions
then having been enslaved by amerikans, must qualify us
for zillions.

THE PRINCE OF KOKOMO

baldheads with dreads

deadlocks: baldheads with dreads
a simulated forest of matted hair sittin
on a head pointed towards popular fashion
red, blue, blonde, cockatoo,
monkey see, monkey do.
clairol dreads
twisted into perfection beyond a shadow
of a meaning. an outback of matted hair
tamed into looking non-threatening
by a mind that automatically copies
but can only fax back imitation minus comprehension
deadlocks: baldheads with dreads
a momentary fixation, destined
to go up like a puff of ganja
the minute a new sensation sets foot in town.
loyal only to vanity,
deadlocks ride on the coat-tail of real dreads
they only dare to lock their hair now that wite folks
say its alright, Essence swears its not ugly,
& the beatings or executions only occur in otha countries.
deadlocks: baldheads with dreads
walk around, twisting their hair in public
the most rebellious thing
some of them will ever do.

LAINI MATAKA

patriotism

i pledge my allegiance
to God and humanity
to never kill anotha
except in defense
of my life, or that of
a significant otha, i.e.
the earth.

a day in the life
of osama

not the least bit surprised, i rise
thanking Allah,
i do my ablutions with ancient finesse
in a manner akin to walking on water
i float around the perimeter of my
thirty room estate, affectionately called 'the cave'
i check on all 20 of my wives, to be sure
they're still contained within the confines of my love
i send my children off to the
school of americas
& return to my lair for a lite fare of dates & figs
when the sun's noon-day drippings, shed untainted light
throughout my domain
i check america's most wanted list
to see if i've been captured yet.
if it's tuesday or thursday, i go to dialysis
otherwise, i watch re-runs of FARENHEIT 911 till
dinnertime; then, i eat
a simple meal of kentucky fried goat
& madea's collard greens
at sundown, i'm off for my daily jaunt to the u.s. embassy
everybody knows me there, so i just float right on through
i try to turn myself in, but the officer in charge refuses
we laugh
later on, georgie-porgie & i hookup
for some all-night dancing at club haliburton
that rascal sure knows how to party.

LAINI MATAKA

all i kno about
unions

my tongue, my nipples and my sugar walls
all
took part in the strike against yr touch
it was my clit
                                    that turned scab.

the burning glow of sisterhood

i have bled with u too often, cried for u too much
luv'd u so flagrantly
i actually believed my wanting it so
cld free u
to uncover yr face, take a seat in a classroom,
or seek contraceptives.
u're so embedded in my consciousness
having breasts has made me dauntless
in my pursuit of yr right
to paint yr toe-nails red/& feed yr child from
tits fashioned for just that, anywhere, anytime.
with a mother superior's passion,
i've prayed for yr delivery from the evils of
daughter drownings, child/bride horror,
suttee flesh burnings, ripped out clits
& men whose touch make u cringe.

i am never cavalier about our capacity for victimization.
a 12 year-old being sold to a rich man
on the otha side of the world, in a country
i never heard of & cant pronounce,
fills me with just as much righteous indignation,
as a child being molested next door.

& just as warring gods send out soldiers to defend
their names/i march heartbeat for heartbeat with u,
in yr silky sarongs, fig-leaves, tie-dyed lappas,
three-piece suits, embroidered kimonos & moo-moos,
kicking and beating on change
which aint nothing but a door, that always opens
when u put enuff pressure on it.

LAINI MATAKA

the burning glow of
sisterhood *(continued)*

menopause has put an end to all that bleeding nonsense
for myself as well as for othas;
my tears have learned to either find a mission or dry up.
i now shoot out projectiles of love, aimed at
all the political jinni, sexist imps & religious demons
that separate my sisters from mirrors
that reflect absolute fulfillment

(even in the dark).

hezbollah, hamas, plo, al-queda, u name it...

No ignorant wrath do I speak of
But a zealously nurtured flame of unvarnished intelligence
Tunneling through generations of shackled psyches
Ever burrowing through the muck & mire of
Israel's right to protect itself with
Red, white & blue arms,
That blow off the legs of brown & beige children.

There will come a wrath, so pure, blood will be the steed
Drawing it's chariot/galloping up a stench
It will sweep across the earth, a mighty scimitar
Slicing away at the garbage of our times,
A prayer in horrific motion
Forcing spirit from bone & devouring it with divine grace.
Nothing the infidels can imagine
Will protect them from their karma
Or the demonic integrity of its intensity.

LAINI MATAKA

911
reflections

somebody kills u like u been killin othas
& u swear eye for an eye vengeance,
but when we talk about reparations
u pluck out yr eyes like Oedipus
& hitch a ride on the Alzheimer's Express.

2

thousands of people didnt make it home
yesterday, their families must've felt
the same way afrikan families felt
when we didnt make it home either

3

it was on every station
the death & destruction made new york
look like a foreign country
in the wake of amerikan intervention.

4

twin towers fell
& in the families of
each individual
gaping holes appeared.

5

nobody deserves to die like that
neither did those people
in the bottom of those ships.

6

since i dont
kno how

i have
never
celebrated carnage.

7
just as i wldnt raise
my glass to toast amerikan
deaths, i wldnt
dance a jig
over the deaths,
of foreigners either.
the violent extraction
of life, from itself
will never find me
rejoicing.

8
when the party was jumpin
u heard us banging at the door
butchu wldnt let us in
& as the food started disappearing
& the drink ebbed in its flow
u invited some of us in, to have
whatever the sorriest of y'all didnt want
& now that some thugs have crashed the party
u want us to come in & engage them
while u sneak out the back door
with the blk gold.

LAINI MATAKA

happy birthday, mama

(FOR DARCENDA WILLIAMS)

thank you for my breath, from baby sweet to now
for the blood that dances and sings all through
me, so glad to be, a part of you.
thank you for my doe eyes, always watching
always wondering. and the freckles sprinkled like brown sugar
all over my face. thank you for the way
my hips move as if there's music when the real vibration is
the rhythm i inherited from you.
thank you for this head full of hair that has always made
people stare, without knowing why. and for this smart mouth
that poetry keeps falling out of, thank you for the intelligence
that makes thoughts grow wild like herbs that
would heal people if they werent so afraid of wholeness.
thank you for my common sense like radar/the nonsense it
helps me to avoid. thank you for my ability to love
endlessly and fearlessly, over and over again.
thank you for my courage in fighting abuse from the tiniest spark
to the most destructive blaze.
thank you for wanting me, nursing me
surrendering me, thinking about me, missing me,
and loving me/even from a distance.
whether life turns out to be just like/or nothing like
the picture i tried to paint
the song i wanted most to sing
or the poem i was living only to write
thank you so much for opening life's door
and letting me in.

THE PRINCE OF KOKOMO

naughty by nature/
but not really

by nature it wasnt his preference
as a youth, he'd been converted
by some orange jump-suit wearers
that his best chances for sustained life
were ensconced between his cheeks.
he never had the privilege of choosing
between waking up with his beard
on her face, or
a beard in his face.
from years of practice,
he learned to hate what he was
and loathe what he was not;
he didnt see himself as gay
just acted that way.
too bereft of masculine memories to change
back into...
he luv'd no one, nowhere, no time .

2.
she taught him to pee sitting down
burned all the signs, markings and maps
that might lead him to manhood.
she strived, like an inept god to make him
into her own image.
he had a delicate constitution.
the neighborhood punked him
outa his ballet slippers and
conspired with auntie to twist him into something
they cld all reign superior over in comparison.
everyone from his teachers to his preachers,
said he'd grow up to think pink,
& not wanting to disappoint,
he did.

LAINI MATAKA

naughty by nature/
but not really *(continued)*

3.
saying he was
made everything easier.
made his parents stop harassing him
about marriage;
made his sister stop tossing her shark-infested
friends at him.
made his uncles stop trying to macho him
into shooting something between the eyes.
made his brother stop speaking in public.

never having discovered a place where he cld be
feigning queerness allowed him
all the opera he cld absorb; he cld
prepare a pheasant under or over glass.
cld operate a flower shop in a mall
dress only for scandal
& send any woman on her way, with a flick of the wrist.
the most popular definitions of manhood
were a size nine, and he was a size seven.
so it was just easier
to say, "gay".

4.
exclusion is not a valid reason for inclusion
into a group that suffers for what it was
born to be.
there's enough bad press & mysticism surrounding people
who can vibrate on both male & female frequencies;
they dont need to be mistaken
for those who weren't born gay,
but became…because.

THE PRINCE OF KOKOMO

black feminist
by default

as if his chauvinism hadn't spawned her feminism.
the insecure man accuses
any blk woman who wont kiss his behinds
or suck his dick,
of being a blk feminist

for a blk man entrapped in a wite man's shadow
any blk woman who wont agree with him
or surrender her brain for his shaping
is a blk feminist

to a blk man on the verge of extinction
any blk woman who wont abandon herself
to create a vacancy for him
is a blk feminist.

for a blk man who didn't get enuff tittie milk
any blk woman who wont let him have his way
is a feminist. something u give a beat down
and then flee from on teeny, tiny feet.

LAINI MATAKA

opening of the museum of the amerikan indians

1.

they came from the lowest and the highest points
of this hemisphere.
letting memory lead/they followed the steps of
ghost dancers, still iridescent
from the glow of a lifestyle
that has played possum,
for hundreds of tearstained years.

2.

they marched like stars staking out
their place in the heavens.
the spirits of their contributions
came rising up outa the earth like turquoise steam
clustered in groups like assorted gemstones
they raised the vibration of peace to such an extent
only a tsunami or some such, cld bring it down.

3.

they swept the sky with feathers
breast-stroked the day with gold & amethyst
fed the hungry far beyond what their minds cld digest
dazzled the hours with glimpses of vintaged gods
& star-impersonating goddesses
that wept openly to be so proudly unveiled.

4.

all the statistics i had on them
evaporated in the heat of a purging sun.
there was no alcohol dripping from their feathers
no diabetes lurking in their moccasins.

no domestic abuse reflecting from their leggings.
no hatred painted on their faces.
nothing but love, such an all-knowing virginal love
it had to be protected.
so,
the ignoble savages
were roped off to the sides
in a humongous attempt
to keep them from infecting
the Natives,
     again.

LAINI MATAKA

boy meets
girl

i met him at a conference
we flirted with the same sessions
posed aloud, the same questions
till finally, i agreed to lunch
so i cld pick his brain/which turned out
to be quite an abundant place.
as part of dessert, it was only natural
for him to ask me out
which i refused,
becuz he was wite & aint no monsters
havin' no ball up in here.

the concrete madonna

still lookin good
the oldest tart in the world
stands
in the middle of the harbor
begging the world
for its tired & poor
to crush into mush
to feed her retarded son,
sam.

LAINI MATAKA

this little
piggie

this little piggie wants iraq
this little piggie stays home
this little piggie bombs palestine
this little piggie screams shalom
this little piggie cries hee, hee, hee
all the way to the bank.

madonna auditions
for madea

madonna said
she looked into that little blk boy's eyes
and they made a connection.

the queen of never was a virgin
having somehow blown the opportunity for a colorful birth
has been working the fringes of melanin all her life;
delusions of exotica dancing in her head
she discovered Alvin Ailey whose expertise
allowed her to peek through a window into blk world
to see what she'd been missing,
next thing u kno, she was in a video
sleasing around in a baptist church setting
blk choir wailing in the background while she & Leon
did their mating dance.
but that didn't lessen the longing to be blk
so her personal life took on more notoriety
than her performances.
she screwed Dennis Rodman's brains out
till he was so conflicted
didn't kno whether to suit up or don a wedding dress.
now she's gone slumming in Malawi &
found herself a blk baby.

she said
she looked into that little blk boy's eyes
and they made a connection.
what kind of connection, like madonna & child,
mistress & slave, owner and pet?
or did she feel a connection between her wealth & his poverty?
customized viruses & demonic economics
killed the child's mother & other siblings.

LAINI MATAKA

madonna auditions
for madea *(continued)*

the father was so traumatized; he let her take his remaining son
not to keep forever, but just till he cld get back on his feet.
he didn't kno her intentions, he thought she was a humanitarian
& she must've thought he was a fool,
becuz healthy Afrikans do not give away their children.

she said
she looked into that little blk boy's eyes
& they made a connection.
something her immaculately wite conception denied
cld be symbolically had/by taking possession of a blk soul.
she had no problems separating that child
from every blk influence in his life. even went so far as
to invite others to visit that same country where she
guaranteed they wld be moved to charity.

if she cared anything about Afrikan people, she cldve sponsored
one of the father's dreams & became a part
of the solid ground under his family's feet.
if she wanted to take the child to the
wild, wild west/she cld've offered the father
a live-in job on her estate, thus pulling both of them
up out of the pit, wite supremacy
cast them into.
wite folks cant bestow charity on Afrikans
becuz everything they give, they already owe.

and she said
she looked into that little blk boy's eyes
and they made a connection.
she was thinking, "oh, I've just got to have you…"
he was thinking, "yeah, that's what yr ancestors said…"

THE PRINCE OF KOKOMO

what lost was,
circa 1959

jazzy
that's what they ustah call her
all shimmied up and sequined down
hair finger-waved by jesus
booty defying latex
wiggling
                    anyway.

jazzy
that's how everyone saw her
always at the right place at the
right time. sportin men
who cldnt decide whether to pimp
her or call her
madam.

jazzy
lived like her tail was on fire
till it was. and the dregs that came after
humped with eyes ransacking
every corner of the room
they squirted acid
sucked out her marrow
& swapped it for a deuce on the street.

jazzy
is how she now thinx of herself
moseying down the street,
in clothes crazy enuff to testify.
powder caked on her face
like she makin masque. eye-make-up

LAINI MATAKA

what lost was,
circa 1959 *(continued)*

that amuses or scares. her hair aint seen
a comb since she lost her marrow
& deep inside her eyes,
there is always the threat of a mutiny.

jazzy
is what they ustah call her
now, they only whisper it
behind her back
afraid to be heard, identified
& turned into obsidian.

claiming what
u deserve

waiting for luv
is like having the heart on lock up
& just when u're down to yr last bit of pining
someone comes: looks like, feels like,
talks like the rippling, muscled thing u been
dying for; but
u don't wanna come up outa yr receptive posture
too soon,
so u lean over to get a better look at this person
(with the sun, moon & stars stuffed in his back pocket)
& yr butt raises up off yr seat ever so slightly
like u wanna break/but remembering yr worth
u push yr back, back up against the chair
u reposition yr behinds for a longer spell
& u make the warrior sundance a little longer.

LAINI MATAKA

burn, baby, burn

(RAP BROWN/JAMIL ABDULLAH AL-AMIN)

they found him guilty,
of still being alive
after all the efforts they'd made
to obliterate any living traces
of those blk men who breathed fire
back at the devils: hell's uppercrust
of the seventies.

they found him guilty,
of trading in his gun for a god they
cldnt recruit.
& for that, he must
die like an old black panther
bludgeoned to death,
on the steps of the nearest mosque.

mad at the source

when you're mad at the
ONE WHO SUSTAINS YOU,
you shove yr childish fists deep, down
into yr spiritual pockets; rejecting
the blessings HE designed for you cuz
they don't look like the ones
you picked outa the catalog;
& when what you receive turns out to be
better than what you requested,
you start feeling all embarrassed, cuz you kno
HE heard u talking smack about him behind his back.
but the ONE WHO SUSTAINS YOU doesn't hold grudges,
& once HE breathes into u, yr account is forever open.
there is not a day within the realm of human experience
that doesn't begin & end without a blessing..

LAINI MATAKA

five foot one & destined to have fun

* (FOR CONVICTED SEX OFFENDER RICHARD W. THOMPSON)

too short for nebraska 's shawshank
he was just tall enuff to convince a twelve year old
to touch his fifty yr-old, filthy, nasty thing.
unless blood is shed, her soul will belong to him forever.

he was just tall enuff to convince a twelve year old
that they were equals & maybe even in love.
unless blood is shed, her soul will belong to him forever
the stain of his touch/her permanent blush.

that they were equals & maybe even in love
if pedophilia can be embellished as such
the stain of his touch, her permanent blush.
for the right little person, there was a dearth of protection.

if pedophilia can be embellished as such
we wonder if the judge was out of touch,
for the right little person, there was a dearth of protection
for that filth/wrapped in skin, too much.

* (The female judge said he was too short for prison & relagated him to house arrest)

THE PRINCE OF KOKOMO

mama binta – mountain eagle woman

where aches do not dare
and bones fear to creak,
she is going
to where color is a sought-after adornment
not an indicator of intelligence
to where dancing is mandatory
and felicity is compulsory,
she is going
to the place her actions have prepared for her,
she is going
in the direction her sun has always pointed to,
she is drifting
making an ethereal entrance to a place that exists only
    to celebrate her
and the life she infused into the tiny planet
she was sent to civilize
many moons ago.

LAINI MATAKA

the funny thing
about aids

if AIDS can be transmitted
by touch,
then
so can
stupidity.

the only thing u might
catch
by touching a person
with AIDS
is a glimpse
of yr own humanity.

must AIDS stare back
at u from a mirror
before u believe?
u dont havta be negative
to come up positive.

june jordan

1.
i wanna say something blacknificent
something equal to her stained glass worthiness
reflected in or out of the sun;
something delicate like a doily,
flowering between sacred needles.
i want something incredible to spill outa my mouth
down my clothes onto the floor, out the door
and into the world till everything, including
wite supremacy, comes to a halt,
while all those she fought for, pause
to be led by her fragrance
to an impromptu party I'm giving tonite
for all the human beings left on the planet.

2.
the pain of oppression.
in yr breasts
is that where u hid yrs, sis?
i made a fibroid out of mine.

3.
a system of breath-taking caves
& hand stitched tunnels
yr heart was a planet
that too many wanted to colonize.

4.
this burning capacity for righteousness
swallowed up her whole life
and she swirled around in saintly humility
blasting machine-gun indictments
down to the last bullet/down to the last good cell.

LAINI MATAKA

DAWG

The wite man says
A dog is a man's best-friend
Since only an unconscious blk man wld
Call himself a dog
An unconscious blk man
Is a wite man's bestfriend.

the 'ize'
have it

it's the trademark of the unmelanized
to see a dollar bill, and get hypnotized
what doesnt turn a profit they ostracize
with their make-believe democracy they mesmerize
all the colored of the world they seek to pauperize
christianize, pasteurize and sodomize
till all things wite they yearn to patronize
still the people of the sun dont recognize
that the wite in their hearts they need to cauterize
their commitment to black they need to notarize
till determination radiates from all blk eyes
our place in the universe we will not jeopardize
by being the poisoned carriers of the pale ones lies
the luv of our children we must dramatize
till their hearts and minds begin to energize
and all the greatness that is us will finally mobilize
with the help of the Most High to civilize
the populations of the world that epitomize
the desire to cleanse and naturalize
by genetically banishing the unmelanized.

LAINI MATAKA

fenty unchained

Turned the nation's capitol into a brothel
A cat-house for developers
A playground for sub-prime lenders
A pervert's home away from home
A school-teacher's purgatory
A decent student's attica
A rich-man's bitch
A poor-man's cross
A home-owner's nightmare
A mutated, albino's paradise.

they want
to be us...

they want to be us
if they cant darken, then
we must be skinned alive
if they cant sing
they we must be made to scream
if they cant dance
then we must be shackled
if our god is omnipotent
then theirs must be diabolical…

LAINI MATAKA

the invisible
ones

we are the invisible ones
the original bones beneath the first flesh
the consecrated center dripping with the essence
of all the Blacks that ever...

we are the invisible ones
we perform ethereal acrobatics of the
highest magnitude/to keep the world/wide computer
from deleting the ebony hue right off yr backs
or the coveted melanin right out of yr genes.

we the invisible ones
have been with u longer than birth & almost as long as death
we were the friction that built yr first fire/the notion in yr mind,
to carve the first wheel. our whispers financed yr mathematics
& our love for u planted stone encased miracles across the
        desert
structures so designed for timelessness/that the world wld
        travel
around itself & back again just to see...
what blackness had wrought.

we the invisible ones
have helped u win every crown u've ever strutted around in
have ridden with u into every battle u were surprised to win
we've quenched u through more droughts than u cld record,
when those ships took yr breath/we breathed for u
when yr mind fled/we found it, nursed it & brought it back to u
when u jumped overboard/we caught u.
when u tried to starve/we fed u...
and all we wanted in return was remembrance.

THE PRINCE OF KOKOMO

we are the invisible ones
who sponsor u unconditionally/support u everlastingly
we're not perfect, cant change night into day
but whatever we have at our disposal, we will
use it to restore u to grace, because we need u
we cant maintain our place among the ethers
 if u refuse to acknowledge us
we cant work our mojo, if u wont call on us
we cant be God's emissaries if u wont believe in us.

we are the invisible ones
we carried u like heroes to the other side of slavery
we gave u the fancy boots with the civil rights in them
we pressed yr fist into the black power manifesto
and we blessed u with a sacred Pan to hold all your Africanisms.

we the invisible ones
are not too enchanted with u right now
u keep forcing us to dance out the pain
of unacknowledged miracles.
make us bear witness to yr adoration
of everyone from ugly abe to rev. moon.
u've cut off that portion of yr tongue
that knows how to say our names.
and when we try to come close/ u
treat us like ghosts.

we are the invisible ones
who wait for those of u with cell phones to call on us
for a change (and get a real exchange)
we cld help u more - but our power is directly connected
to yr belief & remembrance.

LAINI MATAKA

the invisible
ones *(continued)*

we've got answers to questions u havent begun to ask.
but u'd rather watch Oprah, ask Dr. Phil, or get a
spiritual reading from some exotically clad infidel with a
Bachelors in Yoruba from aol.com.
we are the invisible ones
sitting on the millenniums as though
they were adinkra stools/we cant survive w/out u
& u will never make it thru the middle of this passage w/out us.
so when u're in a bind, call us. when u're overwhelmed,
give us a holler. when yr pockets are gettin thin, reach
out for us. when u're about to go into luv, ask us. when u
tumble out of luv, lean on us. when u've gotta go to court
retain us. dont write yr councilman, dont search for a chat-
    room,
dont email yr high-school mentor, dont call Tyrone,
yr girlfriends, yr dawg, yr pusher, yr parole officer, or yr shrink.

call us/we aint in the phone book/we're in yr blood
call us/the invincible, the invisible, the inevitable
the only otha power working for u that whitey cant take away
call on yr ancestors/not tomorrow, but today.

to my new neighbors

You
think
you're
amerikan
the way
the jews
thought
they
were
germans.
u
just
wedded
yrself
to
the nastiest
karma in existence.

LAINI MATAKA

so true to the red, white and blue

I AM THE RED

refusing to move beyond the first chakra, pornographic
in my need to castrate, dominate and perpetrate
still bloody from the red skins torn apart by settlers' teeth
my being is trapped in sadistic stripes, cut out of native flesh
that mistook me for human, and gave me food.
i am the red, devoted to the destruction of everything
in my path, including the path itself.

I AM THE WHITE

stars with the color sucked out of them
making them too dysfunctional
to point out a promised land or a trail w/out tears
i am the absence of color
in no way bound to things of color
even the ones that claim to be people.

I AM THE BLUE

born of the cutlass, which only becomes sacred
once it is stained with red. darker than the blue
that regulates the streets by day,
i only come out at night when the enemy has been lulled
to sleep by peace treaties and amendments
that these stars and stripes will never keep.

THE PRINCE OF KOKOMO

straight up

If white people just flat out admitted
To being devils,
Guess how many negroes
Wld be gluing on horns & sewing on tails.

LAINI MATAKA

revelations

(INSPIRED BY HOWARD THURMAN)

u are not God, but
GOD is u on a level
that will deny comprehension
as long as u try to measure
her omnipotence.
u can never be more than God,
but yr every attempt at being godly
will do well to lessen the gap.

GOD is never lost, therefore, any disconnection
lies solely on human shoulders;
for GOD's love, is what gives Gibraltar its steadiness
he is always in yr face while masked by yr face
at the same time.

unlike u, GOD is never petty;
she exists to forgive.
compassion, is the breath that sustains her.
the ugliest of yr deeds put together,
have not reviled her enuff to revoke
all breathing privileges on this planet.

GOD can never be adequately described
his immensity cannot be entertained
especially by a brain operating on 10%
but the heart breastfed by purity
finds no mystery, for it is there
GOD gratefully expresses himself.

THE PRINCE OF KOKOMO

the institute of
karmic guidance

(FOR TONY BROWDER)

Watching in shock from the highest ethers
souls that have loved u the most & asked from u the least
have fired another round of flares, launched another fleet of
    lifeboats
dispatched another band of x-men, to rescue u
from your criminally insane lust to be wite.

royally navigating like Egypt on the Potomac ,
i, the institute of karmic guidance, sail through timeless waters
to reach the shores of your consciousness
where like a divine gardener
i will tenderly fold back the petals of yr
awareness, cleanse the core & stimulate remembrance.
yr respectful grasp of karma, will be revitalized until yr
every thought, word & deed invokes the sagacity of Ausar,
the tenacity of Auset and the purity of Heru.
my presence, even on the minutest level,
will be the only meteorologist u'll need
to decode the what from the who & the when from the whether
mysteries are defined as such by those who don't know.
in a manner known only to myself/the course of yr lives
will be rerouted pass BET, MTV & other 3-letter undoings
the best in you will swell beyond where
babies are the ill-conceived survivors of one-night stands
blk genitalia are market items on e-bay &
blk folks are disgraced, displaced & replaced
wherever they are currently found.
where wite supremacy has u addicted to fear & loathing
i will de-tox u with virtual glimpses of Kemet &
times when people who looked just like u,

LAINI MATAKA

the institute of
karmic guidance *(continued)*

stood at the helm of the ship known as the world.
the light emitted from their faces still passes for clouds.
& that same light is trying to catch a spark in u.
if u'll take my hand, i'll lead u back into yr own future
& with truths more experienced, than written
we'll go toe to toe with the mendacity cross/dressing as history
till the time when all black genes can be certified as
institutes for karmic guidance & indescribable love.

haiti

ever since the Haitian Revolution
the ostentatious cripplers
have been meeting
planning & scheming - lying & wet dreaming;
first in dark rooms, heavily scented with the intertwined
pungency of rum & cuban cigars
now, in the oval office with brandy & a little blow
but ever since the Haitian Revolution
they've been stalking & instigating
patiently dismantling & regulating
to make those Afrikan diasporians pay a thousand
hunger-filled times, for dancing
on the defeated heads of white men.

becuz those black believers had the unadulterated guts
to rear up on two legs & spit the brutalities of bondage
back into the mouths of their persecutors
the butchers
have unanimously agreed to kick Haiti in the gut
every time it tries to rise. to use IMF hands to strangle it
to defile it with a specifically trained army of the insane.
to poison it when it tries to feed itself/to kidnap & terrorize
its administrators when it tries to assert itself.
becuz he who dares to strike out at the 'master'
 must die in perpetuity.

those black beacon-holders didnt just stir up a little dust
when Haiti stood up, it cast a shadow so far
shade was suddenly available to the
enslaved in distant places/ males found their genitals

LAINI MATAKA

haiti *(continued)*

& females started bearing human beings instead of chattel.
folks got to acting uppity, turning into guerillas/which whitey
    always
accused them of being.
the word was out, that the black man was adept at killing
& the white man was amazingly competent at dying.
the successful slave uprising of that tiny nation
brought about a metamorphosis in the very soul of every
black person blessed enough to hear about it.
& the mythological inferiority of the Afrikan crashed
like giant dominoes around the world!
& for that, their right to self-determination is spit upon by
every amerikan administration that fumbles along.
uncle sam is the ringleader in all efforts to destabilize Haiti
& when the dark & beautiful petition amerika for asylum
when they risk their lives for the Dream in boats built for failure
amerika sends them right back home, with a note saying
we cant help u unless u let us pillage u.

& even though the people remain adamant/global warming,
& strange harp music, is now thrashing the country around
beating and stomping on it thug style/while the people most
responsible for the aggressive changes in climate,
suffer the least and care even less.

& that's where we come in/all Afrikans are related
when family members live hundreds of miles away, they dont
stop being family becuz we cant see them & havent met them.
Haiti fought for every blk, brown & tan one of us
& we've got to offer some of that fight back,
whether that means collecting dead presidents

THE PRINCE OF KOKOMO

or exerting direct pressure on live ones.
whether it means boycotting a popular corporation till it lob-
    bies
up some credible aid for the Haitian economy,
or going door to door in our communities on a clothing drive,
we've got to do something, even if it means
sending a small & skillful cadre of workers
down there to help do whatever will bring the most good
to the greatest number of people.
we've got to do something,
even if the most & least we can do is **PRAY**.

livin in lack

As long as you accept crumbs
You'll never have a cake
Let alone a bakery.

notes on
a holocaust

the jews will never forget auschwitz
nor will they allow the world's memory a statute of limitation
they will never talk about the nazis with a sense of
'well it wasnt all of them'.
they will never appear on television
court-jesting about the heat of the OVENS
when they 'blow up', they dont go
lookin for nazis to handle their business
they dont let others interpret
the bloodstains on their history
when they feel threatened
they dont lay on nazi couches seeking
comfort or protection
and no matter what
outrageous acts they commit against others
they always redirect the focus
    back to what was done to them
and it works.

LAINI MATAKA

the power
of prayer

Pain is the name given to the space
Between u and yr creator.
A daily reconnection with the divine
Can abort microscopic fissures before they
Give birth to alienation.

putting my faith
back on

Today I reaffirm my commitment
with my creator
To fly as high as impossible
& with eyes closed against conflagrations
To join the many
who now walk on water.

when u honor a woman,
u honor the earth

with the one and only god looking right over my shoulder
i denounce any scripture & curse
any obscene faith that confers honor on maiming.
i challenge any apparition of holiness to show me the
respect ensconced between assault & battery.
even if it came straight from the king of kings
i cld never ascribe any spiritual value
to hacking off the petals
of a woman's vaginal flower, even when anotha woman's
fingerprints can be found on the knife.

u shldnt even be allowed to think about god
after flinging a can of acid into a young woman's face
becuz she wont leave her youth & family for u.
the hounds of justice shld drag u through the
streets, or at the very least, the women in the
village shld circumcise u, one by one.

only god-resistant men
cld strangle or stab their sisters
for not having the balls
to defend the family's honor against a throbbing
penis bent on punishing her for having a vagina.
a penis that probably prayed at the same
mosque as her revolting brothers, even after
her assault & murder.

the women of the earth are beyond tired of
being bound and unwound by doctrines men
claim to be holy.
why is there never a passage in any of the
holy books that says,

THE PRINCE OF KOKOMO

beating a woman is a cardinal sin
raping a woman is a crime against humanity
killing a woman is tantamount
to shakin yr naked butt in the face of God.

u're on the non-existent side of righteousness
when u claim the prerogative to draw blood from
a woman's face; to gouge out her eyeballs
with yr virtuous fingers becuz u think, not u kno,
but becuz u had some kinda mystical inkling
that she might've committed adultery.
if she sexed all the men in yr village
& left the soiled sheets right on the bed,
u dont have the right to lay one finger on her,
the only thing u have the right to do
is leave.

gouged out eyes, beatings, slashed noses,
these are the just rewards for women whose husbands
got up on the insecure side of the bed, and suspected them
of experiencing somebody else's genitalia.
and if the husband is wrong,
gouged out eyes dont grow back;
chopped off pieces of nose, never find their way back
to wholeness; & beatings never take back their marks
and crawl away shamefully.

this is a shout out from the women of the earth,
we are through with being tied up & tied down by
mythologies, that men claim came from a god
who didnt kno there was a goddess.
the tears of the worlds' women are where rivers were

LAINI MATAKA

when u honor a woman,
u honor the earth *(continued)*

born, & somewhere in those rivers are forgotten deities
yearning for the sounds of their own names, longing to
share their power with their daughters of the dust.
they will not come/unless they are called
they cant be of any benefit/unless they're believed.
so it's for them i speak when i beg of u, mommies
don't send your daughters into the world
to die at the hands of men who only listen to half of what god
     says.
nurse them into the feline warriors their awareness
begs that they be; keep yr cowardice to yrself.
& let them adjust their own skirts
to accommodate their own strides
as they march into the high-ground of the struggle
threatening/only when threatened. warring
only with those who would mutilate their destinies.
let their rejection of global abuse
scream from mud huts to mansions
from projects to palaces,
till men groomed by god, join them in fighting
to restore that feminine principle, from
which all mothers evolved, including the earth.

niggas

How can u deny the existence
of a thing that refuses to die?
If u cant dissolve matter
what's the sense in re-naming it?
How can we bury the N-word
when the N's are still wreaking havoc?
What else can u call an entity
that cannibalizes its young?
We need to stop dwelling on
whether or not to say nigga
& concentrate more on not being niggas.

(& don't act like u don't kno what I mean)

LAINI MATAKA

the digitalized colonization
of information

I will always have books
despite the farenheit 451
intentions of digital technology.
when this brave, new world
is put into place, whose books
will be preserved & kept anew.
julius lester's "look out whitey
blk power's gonna git yr momma?"

Please!

the 411
on the goddess

Giving birth to myself, I leapt out of myself
To demonstrate the wonder of creation
I am the goddess, the mother of all that is
And will ever be.
I am the divine split, out of which living things
Spilled out and populated a world.
For thousands of years,
I was celebrated with rituals resplendent
With words of adoration, hypnotizing music and painted bodies
Dancing feverishly.
My temples dotted the earth like trees, whole lakes
And rivers were dedicated to whispering my name.
I was so un-catagorically awesome
That night couldn't turn into day, without me
Being praised and activated.

Too naked to really be understood,
My followers draped me in a coat of many myths
Like joseph's coat of many colors.
They stretched and molded the reality of me
Into whatever their strengths and weaknesses
Needed me to be.

And then, patriarchy reared its empty head
Making its first act of insanity, the replacement of me
By some male god who didn't even know he was a god
Till he was voted into office.
My existence was outlawed, and my believers were
Tortured and ruthlessly killed.
My temples were desecrated and burned to the ground
Along with the priests who tended them.
And for every assault on my glory,

LAINI MATAKA

the 411
on the goddess *(continued)*

Womankind was trampled to the ground.
That crazy male god, who forgot he had a mother
Wreaked havoc on the souls and minds of human beings
He used his PR network to promote world-wide mayhem.
Women morphed into the fairer sex,
Emotionally strong/mentally weak.
Like children, they needed to be under a man's instruction
In times of war, they were part of the bloody spoils.
Disconnected from the goddess within,
Chinese beauties became victims of the lotus-hook foot,
& for years their feet were so tightly bound
That the bones were forced to grow over top of each other
Making walking superfluous.
As the goddess within was terrorized,
Indian women lived in dread of their husbands dying, because
When a man died, his wife was forced to throw herself
On top of his burning body.
West Afrikan women armed themselves with knives
And declared war on their own clitorises.
European women tried to make themselves invisible
Lest they be declared witches and burned at the stake.
Once violated, Muslim women were driven away from their
        children for allowing the violation to take place.

Though I, goddess was once so voluptuous,
So earthy, so adored, so worthy of creative myths
The present now holds me hostage,
In the deepest caverns
Of every woman's identity;
Won't somebody, somewhere, stand before a mirror
And set me free.

THE PRINCE OF KOKOMO

from nipple
to nipple

from pink dawn to midnight blue, i nursed.
the flower that bore me, let me suck her nectar
several times a day, & all motion in the world stopped,
as she paused, to interact only with me.
my miniscule fingers wld stroke the infinite silkiness of the
spherical flesh/ heavy laden with my life-juice.
my pure, sweet white honey, bio-chemically designed to
flow whenever my need vibrated.
and several golden times a day,
i pulled in life with petulant lips, drew into myself, the
liquefied rock of ages, that flowed up like the nile
from my motha to my grandmotha
and all the grands before.

that unrefined mammary juice that all cultures
bowed down to was mine for the sucking
several blessed times a day.
and one morning when the sun refused to
make the shadows dance across my wall
the song that hunger made me sing, burst outa me,
and the only hands that meant anything to me
reached for me/my anticipation of the tit became other-worldly
when my head hit the bed
i turned my lips towards heaven, but hell
stuck its tongue in my mouth instead.
something cold, mis-shapened, and hard,
was all my hands cld feel.
my eyes burned when i cld no longer see a face
a cold draft of air swept over me, becuz
there was no body there to block it.
there was no flesh to feel along with my meal

LAINI MATAKA

from nipple
to nipple *(continued)*

the breath that always danced with mine,
had left me hyper-ventilating, alone.
the enveloping smell i'd learned to wrap up in
                                        was ghost.

my face flashed ugly crimson,
as i rejected with all my being, the phallic thing.
i raged till everything in my body hurt.
i filled my own ears with it, so i
didn't hear them when they whispered colic.
they spiked my milk with something terrible
poured it into the cold, hard thing
and made me drink it,
pinched my nose till i did.
i choked so hard, thought i was gonna die.
i went to sleep immediately, just to get away from them.
when i woke up, titty of life was back, and
i bit it gumlessly, frantically,
chirping like a traumatized cricket...afraid
i'd never get enuff again

but the next day they tricked me again,
brought back the fake nipple, tasting of rubber
devoid of even the simplest human attributes
this time i held my breath and took it
cuz i didn't want them to make me drink the terrible
stuff again. i knew the days of
warm smelling, soft feeling white honey, were gone,
cuz otha hands started feeding me with the hard, cold
thing. they put me down on something, propped the thing up
with a pillow, and left the room.
i was alone, and there wasn't a heart beating

THE PRINCE OF KOKOMO

in the whole world but mine. i had to eat by myself.
in a room stripped of all body heat but mine,
alone, trapped between two mountains, alone
cldnt turn, cld only drink, cldnt even stop to catch
my breath, cldnt let go if too much came in.
the wetness leaked along the side of my face, around my neck
if i moved, the food wld stop.
i didnt wanna eat alone.
my body went rigid and i wailed, but nobody came.
the only sound my ears cld discern was me gasping,
and somewhere far away, i cld hear titty
shushing the milk for wanting to flow
to fulfill its purpose and my need
but it too was being punished.
my mind folded in on itself
i didnt wanna eat alone & i cried
like i was bein beat up and flung around a room.
fifty years later, i'm still eating alone
and still crying.

LAINI MATAKA

he-man
got issues

rugged in a homeboy kinda way
that only the experienced wld challenge
generously chiseled muscles, godly sinewy
body angled so taut, to receive ripples of pleasure
chains of masculinity confine the air
choked with shipwrecked sounds of muffled discontent
everybody at the party aint happy
thousands of demon-seeds jettison
into where no eggs or honor dare.
the body that was so taut, shivers and rises
zips up its pants & swaggers off with
convolutions about manhood still drippin...
the boy he acclimated himself to
lies bleeding from the midnight welcoming
which will make him, scurry home to jesus
or rise, a beast
comparable to the one
currently slouching towards Bethlehem .

alway shot,
never the shooter

Hollywood
shoots us in a negative light
the NYPD
shoots us down in the night
the WHO
shoots us up with AIDS
& we shoot hoops.

LAINI MATAKA

spinning

When life is spinning
Out of control
Think dervishly
& spin back to God.

complacency

Complacency
weakens the constitution
and retards
the evolution
of revolution.
not because I say so
but becuz it's true.

LAINI MATAKA

all from
the one

Everything that is
Shares the same beginnings
Good & evil are fraternal twins
Forever recruiting around their differences.

burying letters

if
burying the n-word
will Take care of niggas
will
burying the c-word
take care of crackas?

LAINI MATAKA

for margaret walker
& her people

for the dimly lit faces, doing what no one records
notes or says thank you for/the ordinary or unseemly
working the underpinnings of liberation
like ants infamously building
consistent in their anonymity.
u are THE PEOPLE that it's always been about
from the nameless who eked out a pinch of food for
runaways, the blood-soaked who wldnt squeal
to the impoverished
who stole from themselves to finance the apocalyptic
dreams of nat, the sheet burning visions of gabriel
or denmark 's recipe for how to snatch a black soul back
from white possession,
in yr daily obsession to stay alive, yr anonymous efforts
carried the race with more intensity and frequency
than the one-time heroes, that history so loves to highlight.

for the soldiers, humpin it from
birth to death, just holding on, taking the insults,
swallowing the venom, that with finesse, erodes a person's
lifeline, false smile by false smile. just holding on,
never seeming to gain new ground
but never giving up any either. holding firm to identity
in the face of multi-million dollar deals that promise
honorary witeness & a plethora of trivialities
that real people cld never need
except in a parallel universe.

for the people who went to court to sport an afro
who called the corporations to the carpet
over braids & corn-rows, who backed the amerikan legal

system up over dreadlocks. i cant promise u
healthy pensions, stock options, or golden years full of abundance
but i do guarantee, my unstoppable, incorruptible loyalty
to the creation of a world replete with the splendor
of nappy hair.

for the uncounted, unnoticed, unrecorded, for those
who were the glue, that moved as we moved, never letting go
nails dug into blackness so deep not even death
cld extract them. for u snatched from
the villages, unmissed, u trampled along on the march,
    unmourned,
u shoved off the ships, uncounted, u dying in the hulls, mute.
for the millions, the snuffed out, silenced, censored millions
existing in time still, not knowing where to go becuz the beacon
u need to see by, can only be lit by yr descendants' remembrance.

for the strange fruit never tasted, for the disappeared
& never seen again, for the raped whose voices were stolen &
preserved on wax by the rapists, for the dis-believed swearing
    yr stories
up & down, to people who hid their ears when they saw u coming,
for the heads that kept to the sky, when there was no human
    comfort
whatsoever to sustain. in honor of yr pain, i cauterize the enemy
within, daring it to ever form again.

for the dreamless, the hopeless, the barren, the abandoned,
    for all the
blk faces lincoln & clinton didnt free, for the sensitive turned
    addict,

for margaret walker
& her people *(continued)*

the artistic turned outlaw, for the genius turned trickster, for the
enchanting, turned whore: I grant u forever access to my
    inner-doors.
for the never had a clue, all those broken up shades of black &
    brown
warring against the invisible thing that kept cannibalizing them.
for the unread, the uninformed, the mystery filled lives
    squashed by
the mystery, the pathologically religious, the too educated to
    make sense,
for the unconscious & their unconscious little ones, for those
who fought unknowingly on the wrong side for all the right
    reasons;
for the politically unevolved & those who never knew
it was all about skin color/the bad feelings they cld never shake,
the boulder they cld never get from under, was all about
    skin color.
for those who knew & lost their minds in the knowing,
isolated, laughed at, ignored for dwelling on
accuracies the enemy cld only refute with violence.

for the teachers severed from schools for not
letting blk youth stumble around in the dark,
for those who lost their jobs becuz they cldn't
get the black outa their blood. for those who'd
go blow for blow with the demons over the
smallest slight, those who were always a menace,
always startin shit, always pushin the limits
of the reality, they attempt
to corral us in.

THE PRINCE OF KOKOMO

for those who refused to believe the hype,
wore blinders, kept on dressing loud, laughing hardy
dancin whenever the muscle in music squeezed them
kept on luvin watermelon, scoffing on chicken,
shrieking out the gospel like thornbirds.
wringing all the joy u cld outa every day,
no matter how little of it u had for yrself
u never surrendered to the notion of there being
anything better to be than yr Nubian selves.

please allow me the honor of wiping clean
the tracks of yr tears. please allow me
the pleasure of serving yr still exalted interests
please drape me with yr acceptance
that it may be my armor & shield
fire up the bevels of yr memory, burn me a sword
of Malcolm X- caliber,
& i will spend the rest of my lifetimes
obliterating yr enemies, till they are no more.

LAINI MATAKA

the duke
of ellington

u kno
i've got it bad when
come Sunday
the only prelude to a kiss
i'm gonna get, is in my mirror
i don't kno what kinda blues I got
just, that it don't mean a thing
if it aint got that swing
but u can bet yr last heartbeat
i aint retreating to no bundle of blues
or sleaze around grieving like a gypsy w/out a song
i'm gonna free-fall into a mellow tone
& start orchestrating the moon's mist
on rainy nights,
when a sophisticated lady such as myself
feels enarmored enough to
throw back her head
& let out a brass tinted Creole love call
u kno a mood indigo
getting ready to seize the Capitol
with a black & tan fantasy
of a new world a comin.

THE PRINCE OF KOKOMO

157

IMF

Int'l mother fuckers
Insidious male fakers
Insatiable maniacs forever
Impious mendacious freaks
Industrious monster farts
Illegitimate mutant foragers
Illiberal maggoty fiends
Inbred misappropriating fools
Imposters most felonious
Ill-gotten malignant funders
Imperial molestation fanatics
Incestuous mutilating frauds

If I was an underdeveloped country,
U cldnt lend me jack!

LAINI MATAKA

progress

progress is not progress
that leads people to level nine
before they're aware of level eight
unless it makes people better in some way
that doesn't hurt them & the environment
it's regress and ought to be followed by egress.

critique on women's month

We gave them
life
They gave us
a month.

LAINI MATAKA

july 4th, 2006

to celebrate
the nation's independence
the district spent 3 million dollars
on fireworks
one for each
homeless person in the nation.

better to sing like a bird, than bray like an ass

(FOR SMOKEY ROBINSON)

What can afrika be to me?
aint no wite women for a bro
to leave his blk wife for
in afrika?

Who wanna go to afrika
when they can look
almost wite in amerika?
go back to afrika,
for what?
a chance to reclaim the core
of my black manhood:
                niggah, please!

LAINI MATAKA

priorities

Michael Vick was responsible for the death
of several dogs/& even after imprisonment
the sports world questioned whether or not
he shld be allowed to return to the game.
catholic priests molest children in double digits
yet they are neither de-frocked or excommunicated
from the church
it must be a source of comfort
for the papal victims to know
justice is blind, unless it's a canine.

the taking
of persia

The first time they did her
they were just sowing radioactive seeds
for future assaults.
they didn't wanna rape her right away
wanted to break her down first
so they got their allies
to help hold her down for 12 years
reducing her access to the basics
(food, medicine, water)
& when she appeared too weak to resist
in front of the whole world
they pulled their missiles
out of their pants
& jammed her in the eyes, ears, nose,
mouth and vagina
& to be sure they had everybody's attention
they turned her over
& clustered her right in the arse.

now that all of her orifices
have been repeatedly desecrated
& contracts have been wrought
to gather her enormous bleeding
the perps zip up their pants
as if they were lifting sanctions.

LAINI MATAKA

intifada

when evil turns out not to be amphibian,
but instead, wears Armani & looks like the boy next door
it must be hunted down like a rabid dog
by a posse carrying torches
or a circle of hearts, carrying virtuosity.
when evil is imperceptible among humans
& beings of light are forced to use darkness
to cloak their might.
when evil seems to be w/out obstacle
& moves with the ferocity of a forest fire
we must all dive deep into our Godselves
& raise the stakes a little higher.

the fight against evil is never beyond reach
angels are muscle in
the arms of the righteous.
as soon as evil steps into yr awareness
attack, if it tries to overpower u
beat & **kick** on it. if it gets u in its embrace
break its skull with yr forehead
if it gets a grip on u, **bite** it.
if it shrugs off yr teeth, **spit** on it!

dont wait till it shows up in a theatre near u
as soon as rumors of evil threaten yr ears
as a part of the living God, it is yr moral obligation
to study that evil like a scientist in a biological warfare center.
& then tell everybody u kno/at least twice.
tell it, until u can run it in yr sleep
tell it, until it rings like a mantra.
tell it, until they put a bounty on yr tongue.
when/ the place where yr dreams gather

THE PRINCE OF KOKOMO

forces one eye to remain open
when evil has ID'd u,
has u & yr convictions wearing dark shades
& peeping out of doorways.
resistance respects the right to flee.
the truth will be better off crossing a border
in yr breast pocket, than ground into a powder
by the boots that seek to stomp u to death
there are so many bunkers on the battlefield
& no honor is lost
in the pursuit of a better one.
but
when flight, like a possibility, has been shot down
& fortune cements yr feet to the present,
where evil claims every space including
the one u occupy: **RESIST**
not becuz that's all that's left to do, but
becuz it's the most that can be done.
RESIST
with every God cell in u,
even if yr body is bound,
even if yr mouth is gagged,
even if yr eyes are blindfolded,
RESIST with the totality of yr being
shoot nuclear spears from the purity of yr heart
& bring evil to its knees.

LAINI MATAKA

want a baby,
try a puppy

When I was a teen
my family always had dogs
one wld leave & anotha wld come
& sometimes, two wld co-exist.
i loved me some puppies
but I lost interest in them when they matured
I didn't have any patience with them,
cldnt understand why they wldnt just do as I sd.
in some ways,
i was like a young girl
with a baby.

prostitute's lament

now that they all
look like us
what are we supposed to do?

LAINI MATAKA

matrimony

Marriage
Can mean the union
Of any two things, but
Only one can make a baby.

THE PRINCE OF KOKOMO

goodness

goodness is the only thing
that always has the right to be
everything else is a deviation.

LAINI MATAKA

afrikans never knew...

afrikans never died till they came to amerika
never knew aloneness as anything other than sickness
never knew rape as anything but an aberration
never knew they were niggas
till they came to america
& tho it seems they've survived the middle passage
how, will they ever survive america.

a mighty, mighty love

(FOR HEATHER AND KWABENA AMPOFO-ANTI)

despite any words, written or spoken to the contrary
i have always wanted to be loved
in that awesome storybook kind of way
that kwabena loved heather.

i want a love
like that ole time religion
the kind that makes u shout or speak in tongues
until yr heart swells to the point of bursting.
a weatherproofed love
that doesn't seek center stage in the sun, just to
fade into mist when rainy season comes.
one whose only agenda is to live forever;
like the timeless love that kwabena gave heather.

i want a love
straight outa neruda's best days
& rumi's most arabesque nights;
something for angels to envy & gods to brag about.
a love that weaves itself into two
& weaves them into one life
stretched across centuries of ecstasy;
light enough to tip maat's feather;
like the phenomenal love that kwabena gave heather.

i want a love
that sounds like jennifer hudson , serves like
serena williams, defends itself like assata shakur,
struts like tina turner & like dorothy height, endures.
a love with nuclear credentials,
& earth shaking possibilities.
capable of welding all good things together;

LAINI MATAKA

a mighty,
mighty love *(continued)*

like the magnetic love that kwabena gave heather.
i want a love
that embraces like spring in the dead of winter
one that sustains w/out waning & nurses w/out complaining
some of that ancient, kemetian, holy-rolly stuff
impervious to pain & suffering/wired in perfection
against fear and separation.
a love that radiates beauty as its sole endeavor
like the unparalleled love that kwabena gave heather.

i have always wanted to be loved
in that deep-down, all-through-time kinda way
that lesser men tell me is a fantasy;
they say I shld come back to them & reality
accept their vinyl when I kno I need leather
and a man to love me
the way kwabena loved heather.

THE PRINCE OF KOKOMO